SHELTERED INSTRUCTION IN TEXAS

Second Language Acquisition Methods for Teachers of ELs

JOHN SEIDLITZ

Published by Seidlitz Education
P.O. Box 166827
Irving, TX 75016
www.seidlitzeducation.com

For related titles and support materials visit www.seidlitzeducation.com.

12.19

TABLE OF CONTENTS

1. INTRODUCTION

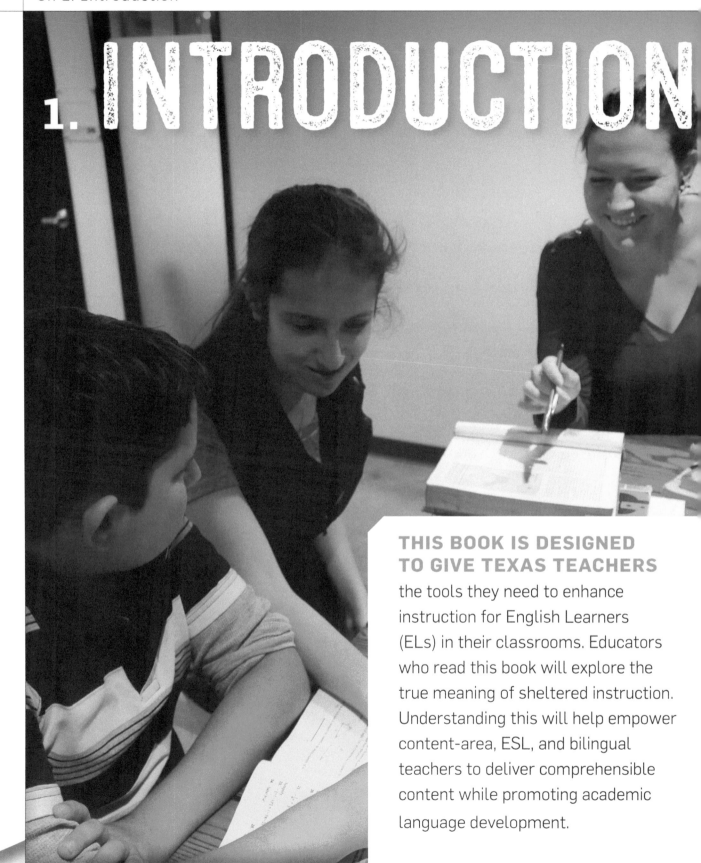

THIS BOOK IS DESIGNED TO GIVE TEXAS TEACHERS the tools they need to enhance instruction for English Learners (ELs) in their classrooms. Educators who read this book will explore the true meaning of sheltered instruction. Understanding this will help empower content-area, ESL, and bilingual teachers to deliver comprehensible content while promoting academic language development.

We will present an approach that integrates English Language Proficiency Standards (ELPS) and TELPAS proficiency levels seamlessly into classroom instruction. This book is based on a combination of research and my experiences with districts throughout Texas over the past 15 years. I used many of the strategies presented while an ESL and history teacher in Floresville ISD. Later, I had the opportunity to work with educational service centers across Texas and the SIOP® National Faculty. In 2010, I had the opportunity to participate in an Institute for Teachers of English Language Learners (ITELL) research project through Arizona State University, where we were able to test the effectiveness of an approach that integrated the *7 Steps to a Language-Rich, Interactive Classroom* and a state's ELPS for 3rd- and 4th-grade classrooms. The outcome of the intervention revealed impressive findings. Students instructed by teachers implementing the approach significantly improved in comparison to students whose teachers did not participate in the intervention.

Since then, we have been able to work with schools across Texas, where we have seen similar gains with elementary, middle, and high school students by integrating *7 Steps to a Language-Rich, Interactive Classroom,* the ELPS, and TELPAS descriptors. Most notably, I am particularly proud of the collaborative work we have done with Alvin ISD, where they have had dramatic gains by implementing this approach at the high school level. Five years ago, the graduation rate of EL students in Alvin ISD stood at 33%. In 2017, 95% of EL seniors in Alvin ISD graduated (with zero dropouts) compared to the all-student district rate of 93% for the same period. Clearly, something special had occurred to provide such a startling improvement! The Bilingual Director, Paula Camacho, and the teachers and specialists who participated in the intervention believe that the change was due in large part because they learned how to give ELs in their classrooms the gift of academic language.

This edition of *Sheltered Instruction in Texas* is responsive to the newest update to the Texas Administrative Code, Chapter 89.B.B (Commissioner's Rules Concerning the Education of English Learners, July 2018). In this edition, the code requires all teachers of ELs to use second language acquisition methods when teaching/supporting ELs. Sheltered instruction is an approach to instruction for ELs that implements these methods. Sheltered instruction will be discussed in detail in the following chapters.

Together with the Seidlitz Education team, I hope that this book will help propel educators of ELs across Texas to empower themselves and their students.

THIS BOOK IS A GUIDE TO HELP YOU:

✓ Enhance instruction for ELs

✓ Explore sheltered instruction

✓ Empower content-area, ESL, and bilingual teachers

✓ Deliver comprehensible content

✓ Promote academic language development

2. WHAT IS SHELTERED INSTRUCTION?

SHELTERED INSTRUCTION IS:

1 a way to use second language acquisition strategies while teaching content-area instruction (Krashen, 1982).

2 content-based English language instruction (Faltis, 1992).

3 a way of providing academic subject matter and linguistic assistance to ELs in the form of visuals, modified texts, and assignments (Echevarria & Graves, 2015).

4 a means for making content comprehensible for ELs while they are developing English proficiency. Sheltered classrooms integrate language and content while infusing socio-cultural awareness (Echevarria, Vogt, & Short, 2017).

What is sheltered instruction and how is it delivered?

The term "sheltered instruction" was first used by Stephen Krashen in 1982 to describe an approach to instruction for second language learners. In this approach, teachers use second language acquisition strategies while delivering content-area instruction. The term "sheltered" originally referred to the language demands placed upon the language learner. "Sheltered language" is language that is surrounded by enough context clues for language learners with sufficient background to be able to understand what is being communicated. In a sheltered class, ELs have a "refuge" from the linguistic demands of the typical mainstream class because teachers will make a conscious effort to provide enough background information and context clues for them to understand the content.

In Texas today, sheltered classes are classes specifically tailored to the needs of ELs. Sometimes these classes are homogeneous and consist exclusively of ELs at similar levels of proficiency. Sometimes sheltered classes are heterogeneous and include ELs at a variety of levels of proficiency. Sometimes ELs and native speakers are together in the same class. Sheltered instruction classes in Texas should always be taught at grade level, and students in those classes should receive instruction based on the TEKS.

What are the characteristics and goals of an effective sheltered instruction model?

There are a variety of models for delivering effective sheltered instruction in U.S. schools. In Texas, some of the more commonly used models include:

- SIOP® (The Sheltered Instruction Observation Protocol)
- QTEL (Quality Teachers for English Learners)
- Project GLAD® (Guided Language Acquisition Design)
- *7 Steps to a Language-Rich, Interactive Classroom* (Seidlitz & Perryman, 2011)
- *Sheltered Instruction in Texas: Second Language Acquisition Methods for Teachers of ELs* (Seidlitz, 2019)

Any sheltered instruction model that is effective will always meet the two main goals of sheltered instruction:

1. **To make content comprehensible to English learners**

2. **To develop academic language**

TEACHERS SHOULD ASK THEMSELVES:

☐ Are the ELs in my class understanding the key ideas of the academic content I'm delivering?

☐ Are the ELs in my class being provided with opportunities for language practice that will help them develop academic language?

If teachers want to know if they are providing quality sheltered instruction for ELs, these two goals can help to provide a framework for answering that question.

Although there is a variety of models of sheltered instruction, researchers have identified some **essential practices** common to each model (Saunders, Goldenberg, & Marcelletti, 2013):

✔ Building on student experiences and familiar content

✔ Providing students with necessary background knowledge

✔ Using graphic organizers

✔ Making instruction and learning tasks extremely clear

✔ Using pictures, demonstrations, and real-life objects

✔ Providing hands-on, interactive learning activities

✔ Providing redundant information using gestures and visual cues

✔ Giving additional practice in time for discussion of key concepts

✔ Designating language and content objectives for each lesson

✔ Using sentence frames and models to help students talk about academic content

✔ Providing instruction differentiated by students' English language proficiency levels

Why is sheltered instruction important in content-area classes?

It is important for content-area teachers to be skilled in delivering sheltered instruction to ELs because they spend most of their school day in content-area classes. In order for ELs to develop English language proficiency, they must receive sufficient amounts of comprehensible input in academic English. The only way for many ELs to receive this input is through high-quality sheltered instruction provided in content areas in English.

When you provide high-quality sheltered instruction to ELs, you fulfill your obligation to ensure that they have the opportunity to master the essential knowledge and skills of the required curriculum. You are also complying with the requirements that are set forth in the English Language Proficiency Standards (ELPS). Most districts require sheltered instruction to be provided to ELs through placement in classes with teachers who have received, and continue to receive, appropriate professional development in this area.

What are the statutory obligations of my role as a teacher of ELs?

Your responsibilities as a teacher of ELs may vary depending on your teaching assignment as well as the program (bilingual or ESL) provided on your campus. However, by statutory reference, teachers of ELs are expected to:

• **Accommodate** materials, instruction, and pacing to ensure that ELs have a full opportunity to master the essential knowledge and skills of the required curriculum. [TAC §89.1210 (a)]

• Address the **affective, linguistic, and cognitive needs** of ELs. [TAC §89.1210 (b) (1-3)]

• Ensure that ELs **participate with their English-speaking peers** in classes such as art, music, and PE as well as all extracurricular activities. [TAC §89.1210 (f)]

- Provide instruction in language arts, mathematics, science, and social studies using second language acquisition methods. [TAC §89.1210 (b) (1)(B); §89.1210 (b)(3)(B)]

- Use knowledge of ELs' **proficiency levels** to instruct, commensurate with EL's linguistic needs, in content-area classrooms. [TAC §74.4(a) (6)]

- Provide **linguistically accommodated instruction** (communicated, sequenced, and scaffolded). [TAC §74.4 (b) (2)]

- Provide instruction that reflects the **cross-curricular second language knowledge and skills** (ELPS). [TAC §74.4 (b) (3)]

- Provide additional supports that are focused, targeted, and systematic to ELs, grades 3-12, at **beginning or intermediate levels** of English language proficiency. [TAC §74.4 (b) (4)]

How can I embrace my role as a teacher of ELs?

From a purely professional standpoint, you can embrace your role by providing learning experiences that enhance ELs' opportunities to acquire the language necessary to succeed on state assessments.

Ideally, all students would benefit from development in both language and content. Under the STAAR testing program, a successful student demonstrates a high degree of grade-appropriate academic language as well as the ability to use elements of critical thinking and literacy (analyzing, interpreting, applying, explaining cause and effect, comparing, classifying, generalizing, drawing conclusions, evaluating, predicting, summarizing, and making connections). Under TELPAS, online reading and listening and speaking tests and holistically rated student writing

EMBRACING OUR ROLES AS TEACHERS OF ELs with a positive spirit helps us create classrooms that "can become cultures where youngsters are discovering the joy, the difficulty, and the excitement of learning and where adults are continually rediscovering the joy, the difficulty, and the excitement of learning. Places where we are all in it together— learning by heart" (Barth, 2002).

collections determine ELs' current levels of proficiency in English (both social and academic language).

But most of us know that teaching is about so much more than results from state assessments. It has been described as a profession, a passion, a challenge, a calling, a service, and an adventure, among many other terms. Your teaching life and your teaching successes are highly affected by your perspective and attitude toward your work.

When we think of ELs as challenges and as students with deficits, we assume a problem/solution stance toward educating them. This is easy to do, especially with the current assessment, monitoring, and evaluation activities that are ever present. But when we allow ourselves to perceive an EL only in terms of a problem, we are setting up a deficit view that can be unintentionally communicated to the student.

When we think of ELs as positive additions to our classes and schools and as students who bring with them their own funds of knowledge and lived experiences, we assume a resource/return stance. We use our resources to provide what ELs need in order to acquire English and academic knowledge. The return on that investment is the development of a successful student by all measures and a valued member of the community.

> Intangibles such as a teacher's attitude toward diverse students, **a belief that all students can succeed** (even if not at the same pace as others), and a commitment to the ongoing social and academic success of each individual student carry great importance.

What are the Factors that Affect Second Language Acquisition?

There are a variety of factors that affect how quickly and efficiently ELs acquire English. Some of these factors are:

> **Motivation**
> **Age**
> **Access to language**
> **Personality**
> **First-language development**
> **Cognitive ability**
> **Quality of instruction**

(Echevarria & Graves, 2015)

Although all of these factors are significant, sheltered classroom teachers only have control over three: motivation, access to language, and quality of instruction. When teaching ELs in a sheltered class, it is important to focus on the factors we do have control over. All techniques shared in this book will help you motivate your ELs, increase their access to the English language, and enhance your quality of classroom instruction.

What are the roles of the cognitive, affective, and linguistic domains in sheltered instruction?

In order to ensure that ELs are receiving the most effective, targeted English instruction in all classes and subject areas, it is important to be aware of the roles that the cognitive, affective, and linguistic domains play in providing sheltered instruction to ELs. Let's look at each one:

Cognitive domain – When we refer to the cognitive domain in learning, we are referring to the body of knowledge that is ever expanding in ELs' brains. Due to its very nature, content-area instruction always involves a wide array of cognitive skills and facts that must be learned. We support the cognitive domain by ensuring that instruction is comprehensible and appropriate to a student's grade level. In order to accomplish this, we use instructional strategies and resources that address ELs' levels of knowledge about a topic. Some ELs will have significant knowledge, while others may have gaps in their learning. As educators, we look for ways to increase ELs' knowledge and understanding of instructional content and materials. We also make sure their academic progress is occurring at a rate that moves them into parity with native English-speaking peers.

Affective domain – The affective domain can be described as the part of the EL's mind that is governed by emotion, stress, and engagement. When a student is dealing with personal issues or is feeling uncomfortable for any reason, their affective "filter" is raised. They are unable to process new information and may feel so overwhelmed that they shut down. To prevent this from occurring in content-area classrooms, we look for ways to provide an engaging and safe learning climate. We also prioritize getting to know each EL as an individual so that we can help them address their concerns and fears about participating in class and making progress. Providing opportunities for low-stress output is essential to supporting ELs' affective needs.

Linguistic domain – As ELs work to acquire increased levels of English proficiency, they use what they know about English, their native language, and the process of learning a language. In content-area classrooms, there is a high expectation for the development of associated academic language. There are certain types of language that are content specific. It helps to make explicit connections between new academic language and general or basic terms applied to the knowledge. For example, when we teach ELs about fractions, we can help them anchor their understanding by connecting the term "fraction" to the concept of "part" or "piece." Encouraging ELs to use new academic language and terms addresses the linguistic domain and advances the ELs' proficiency and confidence in communicating in English.

The chart below offers some "look fors" for the three domains you might note in the classroom setting as well as in other parts of the school.

	A Beginner/Intermediate EL can show success when they are able to...	An Advanced/Advanced High EL can show success when they are able to...
AFFECTIVE	• find their way around campus • follow their daily schedule • work with a partner or in a small group • identify ways in which their culture may differ from the local culture	• seek out help from various staff members as needed • locate and participate in clubs, teams, school committees, etc. • communicate easily with other students • lead small group activities • address any cultural misunderstandings quickly and successfully
COGNITIVE	• demonstrate mastery of knowledge and learning through drawing, sorting items into categories, putting things in order, selecting the correct answer from a limited group of answer choices, or answering a question orally with one or two words/simple phrase • complete assignments that have been shortened or simplified	• demonstrate mastery of learning with grade-appropriate assessments that include some accommodations • respond to questions orally at all levels of thinking, with little to some support • complete the same assignments as grade-level peers or just slightly modified for their level of language proficiency
LINGUISTIC	• use a simple sentence stem to ask for help, respond to a question either orally or in written form, or state an opinion • use a word bank or word wall to complete classwork, participate in groups, or complete a sentence stem • read simplified or adapted text in English or the native language, as necessary	• speak and write in English, with few linguistic accommodations • use more sophisticated sentence stems and language structures in speech and in writing • read grade-appropriate texts for enjoyment and to complete academic tasks • use a word wall, dictionary, or thesaurus as needed to enhance communication

ACTIVITY

1. Create a chart with four columns that show the four messages you want to communicate to your ELs:
   a. **You are important.**
   b. **What we are learning is important.**
   c. **You can do it.**
   d. **We will not give up on you.**

2. Fill out each column with a list of concrete ways that you can communicate that particular message to your ELs. For example, in the first column, list specific ways you can help your ELs realize that they are important members of the learning community. In the second column, list specific approaches to helping students realize that what they are learning is significant to them and to others. In the third column, list ways you can support students in realizing that they are capable of accomplishing their learning goals, and identify ways you can support students who are not feeling successful. In the last column, list ways to create opportunities for students to support one another in the classroom. This can be particularly helpful for newcomer ELs and other beginning level students who are in heterogeneous classrooms.

3. Share your four-column chart with colleagues and periodically review and reflect on your approaches to meeting the affective needs of your ELs.

FOUR THINGS ELS MUST HEAR

You are important.	
What we are learning is important.	
You can do it.	
We will not give up on you.	

WHAT ARE THE 4 ESSENTIAL MESSAGES THAT I NEED TO COMMUNICATE TO ALL ELs?

Messages that ALL students need to hear from their teachers in order to have their affective needs met:

1. **You are important.**

2. **What we are learning is important.**

3. **You can do it.**

4. **We will not give up on you.**

These messages help generate a growth mindset toward acquiring language and learning content. This activity can help you collaborate with your colleagues in planning ways to communicate these messages to ELs.

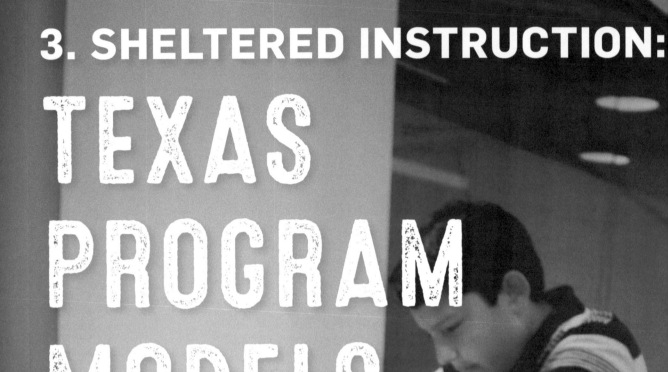

3. SHELTERED INSTRUCTION:
TEXAS PROGRAM MODELS

What is the difference between the terms *program* and *program model* when talking about second language program services in Texas?

In Texas, **two programs** for ELs have been defined and established: Bilingual and English as a Second Language.

ach program has a set of approved program models:

ilingual
rogram
models

- Transitional Bilingual Early Exit
- Transitional Bilingual Late Exit
- Dual Language Immersion One-Way
- Dual Language Immersion Two-Way

English as a Second Language (ESL) program models

- English as a Second Language Pull-Out
- English as a Second Language Content-Based

hat are the goals of the bilingual program in Texas?

cording to TAC §89.1201 (b) and 89.1210 (c)(1&2), the goals of the ingual program and program models in Texas include:

Using their primary language as a resource, ELs will become competent n listening, speaking, reading, and writing in English through the de-velopment of literacy and academic skills in the primary language and English.

ELs will be academically successful.

ELs will participate equitably in school.

four bilingual program models share the same program goals. However, al language program models have these additional goals:

Develop fluency and literacy in English and another language for all students, with special attention given to ELs participating in the program.

At least half of the instruction for ELs is delivered in the students' primary language for the duration of their participation in the program.

Integrate English speakers and ELs for academic instruction, in accordance with the program design and model selected by the school district board of trustees. Whenever possible, 50% of students in a program should be dominant English speakers and 50% of students should be native speakers of another language at the beginning of the program.

Promote bilingualism, biliteracy, cross-cultural awareness, and high academic achievement.

SCHOOL DISTRICTS MAY HAVE ADDITIONAL GOALS FOR EVERY STUDENT IN THE DISTRICT. ELS SHOULD BE EXPECTED TO MEET THOSE GOALS AS WELL.

What are the characteristics of approved bilingual program models in Texas?

Transition Bilingual Early Exit (EE)

> Instruction in literacy and academic content areas is provided in ELs' first language.

> Development of oral and academic English is provided.

> Over time, ELs transfer to all-English instruction.

> Exit typically occurs between two and five years after enrollment.

Transition Bilingual Late Exit (LE)

> Using both the EL's first language and English, cognitively challenging academic work is provided.

> High levels of academic achievement and full proficiency in both languages are promoted.

> Over time, ELs transfer to all-English instruction.

> Exit occurs no earlier than six and no later than seven years after enrollment.

Dual Language Immersion One-Way (DL1W)

> A biliteracy model for ELs integrates language learning with content instruction.

> Academic subjects are taught in both languages.

> At least half of the instruction is delivered in the student' primary language for the duration of the program.

> Full bilingualism, biliteracy, and cross-cultural awareness are emphasized.

> Over time, ELs transfer to all-English instruction.

> Exit occurs no earlier than six years and no later than seven years after enrollment.

> At least half of the instruction is delivered in the student' primary language for the duration of the program.

Dual Language Immersion Two-Way (DL2W)

> A biliteracy model for ELs and English-dominant students integrates language learning with content instruction.

> Academic subjects are taught in both languages.

> At least half of the instruction is delivered in the non-English program language for the duration of the program.

> Full bilingualism, biliteracy, and cross-cultural awareness are emphasized.

> Over time, ELs transfer to all-English instruction.

> Exit occurs no earlier than six years and no later than seven years after enrollment.

What are the goals of the English as a Second Language program in Texas?

According to TAC §89.1201 (b) and 89.1210 (d)(1&2), the goals of the English as a Second Language program and program models in Texas include:

- ELs will attain full proficiency in English and will become competent in listening, speaking, reading, and writing in English through the integrated use of second language methods.
- ELs will be academically successful.
- ELs will participate equitably in school.

School districts may have additional goals for every student in the district. ELs should be expected to meet those goals as well.

What are the instructional differences between bilingual and ESL programs in Texas?

The most significant differences between the bilingual program and the ESL program in Texas focus on the languages of instruction, methods of instructional delivery, materials and resources, and goals of the program. Keep in mind that bilingual programming is required in any district where there are 20 students from the same home language, in the same grade level.

In the bilingual program, the ELs' primary language is used for instruction to develop both literacy and academic knowledge. English is introduced and developed based upon the program model. Instructional methods include approaches that are aligned with the way in which literacy in the first language occurs. For example, some languages are very "transparent," meaning there is a high degree of consistency in pronunciation, semantics (word order for meaning), and syntax (grammar system). In these languages, there is less of an emphasis placed on phonics instruction. Generally, if you can say it, you can write it. In contrast, English is considered an "opaque" language, meaning that there is less consistency in the three systems. Instruction in phonics is common to

WHAT ARE THE CHARACTERISTICS OF APPROVED ESL PROGRAM MODELS IN TEXAS?

ESL Pull-Out (PO)
- Can be delivered in a separate setting or within the general education setting.
- ESL-certified teachers provide language arts and reading instruction.
- Exit typically occurs between two and five years after enrollment.

ESL Content-Based (CB)
- Program services are provided in content-area classrooms where English is developed through sheltered content-area instruction.
- Content-area instruction is provided by ESL-certified teachers.

assist students in navigating the sound/symbol relationship.

Most bilingual classrooms are composed of ELs, with some non-ELs present in Dual Language Two-Way models or by parental request. This impacts instruction significantly in terms of grouping, materials and resources, and language-centered activities. In bilingual classrooms, you would expect to see materials and resources in both languages. State-approved instructional materials are provided in both languages.

ESL students may be served in an ESL classroom for part of the day. There may be a wide array of languages represented. These students may also be supported in regular education content-area classes by teachers trained in providing sheltered instruction. ELs in a Pull-Out program model receive language arts and reading instruction from ESL-certified teachers, while ELs in a Content-Based program model receive language arts, reading, mathematics, science, and social studies instruction from ESL-certified teachers.

ELs in the ESL program receive instruction intended to develop their English language proficiency and their content knowledge.
English is the language of instruction. If the primary language is used instructionally, it is for a specific purpose and serves to bridge understanding of a concept or term. ELs in an ESL classroom may use their primary language in speaking with one another as they complete tasks or to receive peer assistance. Materials and resources in an ESL classroom should include choices from each language of the ELs, but state-approved instructional materials and resources are in English.

Both the bilingual and ESL programs in Texas have as a stated goal of the program the development of proficiency in English to a level that ensures academic success. Bilingual program models also have as a goal the development of the primary language to varying degrees. Dual language program models also state goals of full bilingualism, biliteracy, cross-cultural awareness, and high academic achievement.

How does sheltered instruction fit into the different Texas program models?

Each program model in Texas can incorporate sheltered instruction in a variety of ways. The following chart explains the role of sheltered instruction in different settings within each program model.

Program Model	Role of Sheltered Instruction
Bilingual classes taught in English	Sheltered instruction used to facilitate acquisition of social and academic English
Bilingual classes taught in native language	Sheltered techniques can be used to help students acquire academic proficiency in their native language
Content-area classes	Sheltered instruction techniques make content-area instruction comprehensible for ELs while developing ELs' academic vocabulary.
ESL classes	Sheltered techniques can be used to help ELs acquire proficiency in English academic language used in content-area classes

MATERIALS AND RESOURCES IN AN ESL CLASSROOM SHOULD INCLUDE CHOICES FROM EACH LANGUAGE OF THE ELS, BUT STATE-APPROVED INSTRUCTIONAL MATERIALS AND RESOURCES ARE IN ENGLISH.

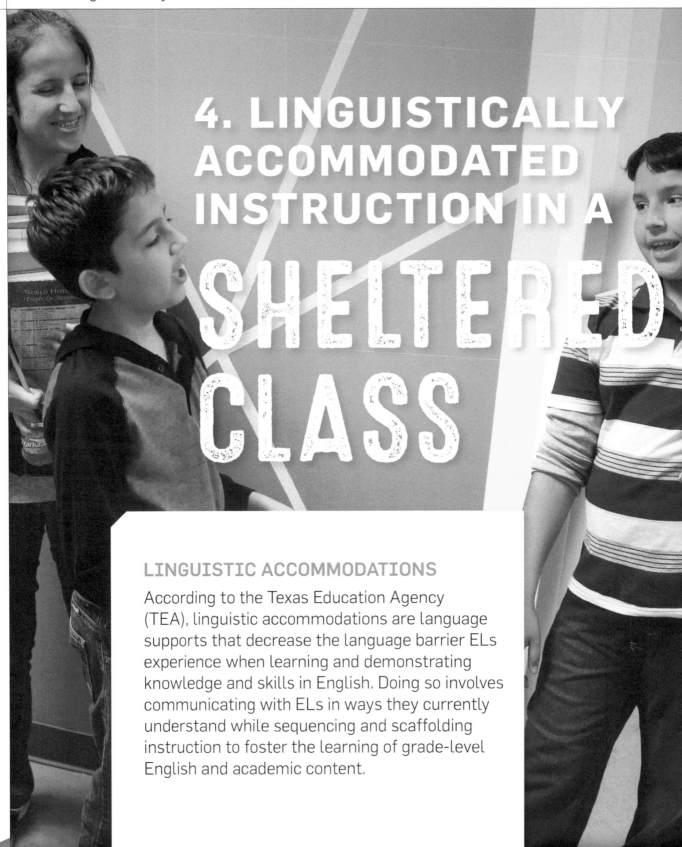

4. LINGUISTICALLY ACCOMMODATED INSTRUCTION IN A SHELTERED CLASS

LINGUISTIC ACCOMMODATIONS

According to the Texas Education Agency (TEA), linguistic accommodations are language supports that decrease the language barrier ELs experience when learning and demonstrating knowledge and skills in English. Doing so involves communicating with ELs in ways they currently understand while sequencing and scaffolding instruction to foster the learning of grade-level English and academic content.

Who determines the accommodations provided to ELs?

Instructional accommodations for ELs are most often determined by the classroom teacher. The LPAC may recommend certain accommodations based upon subjective teacher input from previous years' teachers. In addition, other specialists or administrators may require certain accommodations to be routinely provided; for example, the use of language objectives, sentence stems, and visuals may be the norms or expectations for all teachers, even though they are considered instructional accommodations for ELs.

In the case of assessment accommodations, the LPAC is responsible—in consultation with the classroom teachers—to determine which, if any, of the approved assessment accommodations will be provided to an EL during the state assessments. These decisions are documented and maintained in the student's record. Any accommodation that is provided in a state assessment must be routinely used and requested by the student throughout the year.

For ELs served by Special Education, the LPAC and ARD committees work collaboratively to make these important decisions. The ARD may determine that an EL served by Special Education requires a modified curriculum or modified assessments. Modifications are different from accommodations in that they alter the required curriculum or the assessment. Instruction and assessment may be conducted at a lower grade level and/or the learning expectations may differ from those for the grade level or course. In the case of modified assessments, TEA has determined that these are not considered general assessments.

Texas teachers are required to provide linguistic accommodations to ELs. **TAC Chapter 74, §74.4(b)(4) requires** that Beginning and Intermediate level students receive intensive, ongoing English language development that is focused, targeted, and systematic.

What are the characteristics of ELs at the Beginning and Intermediate levels of English proficiency?

The listening, speaking, reading, and writing skills for students at the Beginning and Intermediate levels of language proficiency are described in the TELPAS Proficiency Level Descriptors (PLDs). The following chart summarizes these skills in a general way; however, these summaries are not appropriate to use in formal TELPAS rating activities.

SUMMARIES OF ELPS: Proficiency Level Descriptors

Level	Listening (d1: K-12) The student comprehends...	Speaking (d2: K-12) The student speaks...	Reading (d4: 2-12) The student reads...	Writing (d6: 2-12) The student writes...
Beginning **(A)**	1A(i) few **simple conversations** with linguistic support 1A(ii) **modified conversation** 1A(iii) few words, **does not seek clarification,** watches others for cues	2A(i) using **single words and short phrases** with practiced material; tends to give up on attempts 2A(ii) using a **limited bank of key vocabulary** 2A(iii) with **recently practiced familiar material** 2A(iv) with frequent **errors** that hinder communication 2A(v) with **pronunciation that inhibits communication**	4A(i) little except recently practiced terms, **environmental print,** high-frequency words, **concrete words represented by pictures** 4A(ii) **slowly, word by word** 4A(iii) with very limited sense of English structure 4A(iv) with comprehension of **practiced, familiar text** 4A(v) with a need for **visuals and prior knowledge** 4A(vi) modified and **adapted text**	6A(i) with **little ability to use English** 6A(ii) **without focus** and coherence, conventions, organization, or voice 6A(iii) labels, lists, and copies of printed text and **high-frequency words/phrases,** short and simple, practiced sentences primarily in **present tense with frequent errors** that hinder or prevent understanding
Intermediate **(B)**	1B(i) unfamiliar language with **linguistic supports** and adaptations 1B(ii) unmodified conversation with **key words** and phrases 1B(iii) with **requests for clarification** by asking the speaker to repeat, slow down, or rephrase speech	2B(i) **with simple messages** and hesitation to think about meaning 2B(ii) using **basic vocabulary** 2B(iii) with **simple sentence structures** and present tense 2B(iv) with **errors** that inhibit unfamiliar communication 2B(v) with **pronunciation generally understood** by those familiar with English Learners	4B(i) a **wider range of topics** and everyday academic language 4B(ii) **slowly** and **rereads** 4B(iii) basic language structures 4B(iv) simple sentences **with visual cues, pretaught vocabulary,** and **interaction** 4B(v) **grade-level texts** with difficulty 4B(vi) at a high level with **linguistic accommodation**	6B(i) with **limited ability to use English** in content-area writing 6B(ii) best on **topics that are highly familiar** with simple English 6B(iii) with **simple oral tone in messages,** high-frequency vocabulary, loosely connected text, repetition of ideas, **mostly in the present tense**, undetailed descriptions, and **frequent errors**

Level	Listening (d1: K-12) The student comprehends...	Speaking (d2: K-12) The student speaks...	Reading (d4: 2-12) The student reads...	Writing (d6: 2-12) The student writes...
Advanced (C)	1C(i) with some processing time, **visuals, verbal cues, and gestures; unfamiliar conversations** 1C(ii) most unmodified interaction 1C(iii) with occasional **requests** for the speaker to slow down, repeat, rephrase, and **clarify meaning**	2C(i) in conversations with some **pauses to restate, repeat, and clarify** 2C(ii) using **content-based and abstract terms** on familiar topics 2C(iii) with **past, present, and future** 2C(iv) using **complex sentences** and grammar with some errors 2C(v) with **pronunciation usually understood** by most	4C(i) abstract, grade-appropriate text 4C(ii) **longer phrases and familiar sentences** appropriately 4C(iii) while developing the ability to construct meaning from text 4C(iv) at a **high comprehension** level with **linguistic support** for unfamiliar topics and to clarify meaning	6C(i) grade-appropriate **ideas with second language support** 6C(ii) with extra need for second language **support when topics are technical and abstract** 6C(iii) with a grasp of basic English usage, and some understanding of complex usage with **emerging grade-appropriate vocabulary** and a more academic tone
Advanced High (D)	1D(i) longer **discussions on unfamiliar topics** 1D(ii) spoken information nearly **comparable to native speakers** 1D(iii) with few requests for the speaker to slow down, repeat, or rephrase	2D(i) in **extended discussions** with few pauses 2D(ii) using **abstract content-based vocabulary** except low frequency terms; using idioms 2D(iii) with grammar **nearly comparable to native speakers** 2D(iv) with **few errors** blocking communication 2D(v) with **occasional mispronunciation**	4D(i) **nearly comparable to native speakers** 4D(ii) **grade-appropriate familiar text** appropriately 4D(iii) while constructing meaning at near-native ability level 4D(iv) at high level comprehension with **minimal linguistic support**	6D(i) grade-appropriate, **content-area ideas with little need for** linguistic support 6D(ii) develop and demonstrate **grade-appropriate** writing 6D (iii) nearly **comparable to native speakers** with clarity and precision, with **occasional difficulties,** and with naturalness of language

These summaries are not appropriate to use in formally identifying student proficiency levels for TELPAS. TELPAS assessment and training materials are provided by the Texas Education Agency Student Assessment Division.

Often, ELs at the Beginning or Intermediate levels of English language proficiency are new to schooling in the U.S., and these designations do little to indicate the educational levels in their native language. In addition, they do not provide information about the academic achievement of these students. With an understanding of student academic/educational background, administrators can make good decisions in terms of placement for cognitive, linguistic, and affective supports.

Note: Beginners and Intermediates may also be classified as immigrants, refugee/asylee students, or U.S. born. Therefore, the rapid acquisition of English sufficient to function in general education classrooms is an immediate goal.

What are the characteristics of instruction designed to meet the needs of ELs at the Beginning and Intermediate levels of English language proficiency?

Linguistic accommodations for students at the Beginning and Intermediate levels of English language proficiency focus on ensuring that students receive adequate comprehensible input. At the Beginning level, teachers allow a "silent period" to let students become accustomed to the sounds and patterns of English, even though the need for silence opposes the demands placed on teachers to accelerate the acquisition of English language proficiency for Beginning ELs (Krashen, 1982).

TAC Chapter 74, §74.4(b)(4) requires that Beginning and Intermediate level students receive intensive, ongoing English language development that is focused, targeted, and systematic. Some students may require support to develop foundational literacy in English and can include such skills as: the alphabetic principle, phonology (sounds of English), directionality of print, translating sounds into writing, and basic sight vocabulary. Many of these skills may not be available in a general educational setting and may require intensive support by an ESL-certified teacher or specialist. This can often be accomplished in the context of an ESL classroom.

The following chart notes the kind of accommodations that are appropriate for students at the Beginning and Intermediate levels. In addition, Advanced and Advanced High levels are shown.*

*Guidelines at specific proficiency levels may be beneficial for students at all levels of proficiency depending on the context of instructional delivery, materials, and students' background knowledge.

LINGUISTIC ACCOMMODATIONS for each Proficiency Level

Sequence of Language Development	Communicating and Scaffolding Instruction			
	Listening *Teachers...*	**Speaking** *Teachers...*	**Reading** *Teachers...*	**Writing** *Teachers...*
Beginning **(A)**	• Allow use of same language peer and **native language support** • Expect student to struggle to understand simple conversations • Use **gestures and movement** and other linguistic support to communicate language and expectations	• Provide short **sentence stems** and single words for practice before conversations • **Allow some nonparticipation** in simple conversations • Provide **word bank** of key vocabulary • Model **pronunciation of social and academic language**	• Organize reading in **chunks** • Practice **high-frequency, concrete terms** • Use **visual and linguistic supports** • Explain classroom **environmental print** • Use adapted text	• Allow **drawing and use of native language** to express concepts • Allow student to use high-frequency recently memorized, and **short, simple sentences** • Provide **short, simple sentence stems** with present tense and high-frequency vocabulary
Intermediate **(B)**	• Provide **visuals, slower speech, verbal cues, and simplified language** • **Preteach vocabulary** before discussions and lectures • **Teach phrases** for student to request speakers to repeat, slow down, or rephrase speech	• Allow extra **processing time** • Provide **sentence stems** with simple sentence structures and tenses • Model and provide practice in **pronunciation of academic terms**	• Allow wide range of reading • Allow grade-level comprehension and **analysis of tasks,** including **drawing** and use of **native language** and peer collaboration • Provide high level of **visual and linguistic supports** with adapted text and **pretaught vocabulary**	• Allow **drawing and use of native language** to express academic concepts • Allow writing on **familiar, concrete topics** • **Avoid assessment of language errors** in content-area writing • Provide simple **sentence stems and scaffolded writing assignments**
Advanced **(C)**	• Allow some **processing time, visuals, verbal cues, and gestures** for unfamiliar conversations • Provide opportunities for student to **request clarification,** repetition, and rephrasing	• **Allow extra time** after pauses • Provide **sentence stems** with past, present, future, and **complex grammar,** and vocabulary with **content-based and abstract terms**	• Allow abstract grade-level reading comprehension and analysis with **peer support** • Provide **visual and linguistic supports,** including **adapted text** for unfamiliar topics	• Provide **grade-level appropriate writing tasks** • Allow abstract and technical writing with linguistic support, including teacher **modeling and student interaction** • Provide complex **sentence stems** for **scaffolded writing assignments**
Advanced High **(D)**	• Allow some **extra time** when academic material is complex and unfamiliar • Provide **visuals, verbal cues, and gestures** when material is complex and unfamiliar	• Provide opportunities for extended **discussions** • Provide **sentence stems with** past, present, future, and **complex grammar** and vocabulary with **content-based and abstract terms**	• Allow abstract grade-level reading • Provide minimal **visual and linguistic supports** • Allow grade-level comprehension and **analysis tasks** with **peer collaboration**	• Provide complex **grade-level appropriate writing tasks** • Allow abstract and technical writing with **minimal linguistic support** • Use **genre analysis** to identify and use features of advanced English writing

These accommodations may be provided in the context of an ESL classroom or through some other intervention mechanism using ESL specialists. When they are not, content-area teachers in general education classes can use sheltered instruction approaches to support ELs at all levels of English language proficiency, including Beginners and Intermediates.

What do the words *focused, targeted,* and *systematic* mean in TAC Chapter 74, §74.4(b)(4)?

The words *focused, targeted,* and *systematic* identify the kind of instruction for students at the Beginning and Intermediate levels of English language proficiency, at third grade or higher. Focused, targeted, and systematic English language instruction is not equivalent to linguistic accommodations in a general education setting. Instead, this language refers to the accelerated English language instruction specially designed for students at the Beginning and Intermediate levels. More information is provided in the chart on the next page.

UNDERSTANDING THE ELPS FRAMEWORK
Foundations of Second Language Acquisition Instruction for Beginning and Intermediate ELs Grades 3-12

Second language acquisition instruction must be:	What is it?	What are some examples?
Focused	**Concentrated effort centered on student acquisition** of vocabulary, grammar, syntax, and English mechanics necessary to support content-based instruction and accelerated learning of English.	• Explicit instruction in English vocabulary and language structures • Lesson plans include cross-curricular student expectations from the ELPS • Use of sentence structures of increasing complexity in vocabulary, grammar, and syntax
Targeted	**Specific goals and objectives** align with vocabulary, grammar, syntax and English mechanics necessary to support content-based instruction and accelerated learning of English.	• Content objectives for ELs align with the TEKS • Language objectives for ELs align with ELPS and language skills necessary for TEKS • Formal and informal assessments align with content and language assessments
Systematic	**Well-organized structure** in place to ensure that students acquire vocabulary, grammar, syntax, and English mechanics necessary to support content-based instruction and accelerated learning of English.	• ELPS integrated into district curriculum frameworks • Comprehensive plan for students in grades 3-12 at Beginning or Intermediate level for integrating language and content instruction • Comprehensive plan for assessing the implementation of focused, targeted instruction for Beginning and Intermediate students in grades 3-12 • Periodic review of progress of ELs through formal and informal assessment

5. PRINCIPLES OF A LANGUAGE-RICH, INTERACTIVE CLASSROOM

IN A LANGUAGE-RICH, INTERACTIVE CLASSROOM, TEACHERS CLEARLY FOCUS ON TWO GOALS: structuring language development and providing opportunities for interaction. Creating and facilitating this type of environment is necessary for ELs because they benefit from a focus on oracy and multiple opportunities to practice social and academic language.

Oracy is the ability to use language skills and structures necessary for fluent and effective communication. Wilkinson (1970) coined the term to highlight the importance of establishing listening and speaking as essential skills that are "parallel to literacy" (Meiers, 2006). It requires teachers to pay explicit attention to specific language instruction so students can comprehend and express ideas in a variety of contexts. In addition, teachers must focus on providing students with multiple opportunities to practice and apply these learned skills. Dialogue must be included as an essential skill in order to expand the grammatical complexities of speech and vocabulary for ELs (Escamilla et al., 2010).

To create a language-rich, interactive classroom, educators must have a philosophy of instruction that promotes academic language and literacy development through meaningful interaction.

Total Participation of All Students
What does total participation involve?

Total participation requires the inclusion of all students in the classroom, regardless of their language level or ability. Teachers must remember that students learning rigorous content and academic language to meet high academic standards in a second language require specialized instruction to do so. Along with techniques such as visuals and hands-on activities, teachers must make a conscious effort to make the learning understandable through a variety of means. It ensures that "every student, during every activity, is involved in listening, writing, speaking, or reading" (Seidlitz & Perryman, 2011, p. 98). Total participation has two essential components that make it successful: comprehensible input and comprehensible output.

In *Sheltered Instruction in Texas: A Guide for Teachers of ELs,* **THE FOLLOWING FOUR PRINCIPLES (T.I.P.S.) FORM THE FOUNDATION OF THE SHELTERED CLASSROOM :**

Total participation of all students

Incorporating academic vocabulary

Promoting literacy and language development

Scaffolding for all language levels

Adapted from Seidlitz & Perryman (2011)

What is comprehensible input?

Comprehensible input is any written or spoken message that is understandable to a language learner because of the context. The phrase "comprehensible input" is part of Stephen Krashen's theory of second language acquisition. According to this theory, humans learn a new language primarily by receiving new messages in language that they understand because of the context. Krashen believed that input is best received when it is slightly challenging for the language learner. If the input is not challenging at all, no language development would occur. If it is too challenging, the language learner wouldn't understand the message. Being immersed in a language you don't understand is not an example of comprehensible input, but incomprehensible input. Instead, learners should be exposed to language that is slightly challenging and engaging. This is referred to as "i + 1," which means "input plus one." Spoken or written messages in the target language should be slightly above the level of the student.

What is the difference between learning a language and acquiring a language?

Language learning involves studying and memorizing the vocabulary and grammar of a target language. Students produce written and oral language and receive feedback from an instructor.

Language acquisition involves receiving copious amounts of comprehensible input with low stress opportunities for output in a target language. The only way for students to achieve high levels of fluency in a target language is by receiving sufficient amounts of oral and written input, with opportunities to express themselves orally and/or in writing in authentic contexts. It is not possible to achieve proficiency by studying vocabulary and grammar alone.

What is the role of the affective filter and why and how is it related to comprehensible input?

The affective filter is a key component of Krashen's model of second language acquisition. It has been described as "an imaginary wall" between a language learner and new input. The wall consists of negative motivational and emotional factors that interfere with a person's ability to receive comprehensible input. For example, if a person is feeling embarrassed and stressed about having to speak aloud in front of his/her peers, it would be hard for him/her to receive comprehensible input. **To receive input, the language learner needs to be relaxed and concentrating on meaning and not on form. The more they are in a state of "flow" and are concentrating on the message, the more input they receive.** The more stressed they are, the less input they receive. This is why it is important for teachers of ELs to ensure that they take steps to lower the affective filter of their students.

How do I lower the affective filter for my students?

To lower the affective filter, teachers must create a low anxiety classroom for ELs. To do this, they need to help ELs feel comfortable making mistakes and taking risks in using English.

What are best practices for providing comprehensible input for ELs?

There are two sources of comprehensible input for ELs: spoken aural (heard) and written. We will discuss each of these in turn.

Aural comprehensible input can be provided by you, by other students in the class, and by media. In order for students to receive effective aural comprehensible input from you, it is important to provide enough context while giving instructions and explaining academic concepts. The SIOP model recommends simple practices that help teachers provide comprehensible input during instruction, such as simplifying speech, clearly explaining academic tasks, using speech appropriate for students' proficiency levels, and avoiding the use of idioms and regionalisms.

To receive aural comprehensible input from other students, ELs need to interact frequently with native speakers and other ELs at higher levels of language proficiency in a variety of authentic contexts. Structured, scaffolded activities where stems are provided can help students participate in conversations where they can receive "negotiated input" (i.e., clarification of English words and phrases that they do not understand).

To receive input from media, it is helpful to find high interest sources. For example, television programs, music, and videos can be helpful. When watching video, many language learners find that they receive more aural input when the closed captioning is turned on so that they do not miss specific words and phrases used in authentic context.

SOME THINGS TEACHERS CAN DO TO LOWER THE AFFECTIVE FILTER INCLUDE:

- Avoiding public correction of errors

- Not forcing students to speak before they are ready

- Allowing ELs to seek clarification in their native language

- Providing feedback on language production ONLY at the student's level of language proficiency (e.g., providing beginning ELs writing feedback that targets the kind of language Beginners produce, not Advanced High students)

- Providing frequent opportunities for peer interaction

- Creating a welcoming, culturally responsive classroom environment

- Getting to know the students' parents/ guardians and maintaining an open relationship with them

Written comprehensible input can also be provided from a variety of sources. The most effective source of written input comes through programs where students read self-selected texts in the target language. In addition, teachers can make classroom texts more comprehensible by making sure that students are provided with sufficient context and native language support to be able to understand the key ideas presented in the text.

Why is providing comprehensible input one of the most important factors in second language acquisition?

Without comprehensible input, language development does not occur. Students must receive sufficient comprehensible input before they will be able to spontaneously produce real output in a target language. It is crucial that all teachers of ELs understand how to effectively increase comprehensible input so that their students will more quickly advance in language proficiency.

What is "compelling input" and why is the concept important?

Compelling input is a term Stephen Krashen uses to describe input so interesting that the language learner forgets that it is in a different language. The learner is relaxed, engaged, and focused on meaning. In a sense, the student is in what is referred to as a state of flow (Csikszentmihalyi, 1990). Flow also happens during reading when students seem to be "lost in a book" (Nell, 1988) or in what Nancie Atwell (2007) refers to as "The Reading Zone."

In order to provide compelling input, teachers must make sure they provide listening and reading experiences that are highly engaging and interesting to the students, and that contain some input that is at and slightly above the students' current level of language proficiency.

What is the role of comprehensible input in sheltered instruction?

Sheltered instruction is a term coined by Stephen Krashen to describe instruction that makes use of large amounts of "sheltered language." Sheltered language is language that is surrounded by context. There must be sufficient context in order for a language learner to receive some comprehensible input. **In a sheltered class, teachers are very deliberate about using sheltered language when giving instructions and explaining academic contexts, and they provide the students with texts that they make accessible and comprehensible for ELs.** They also provide classrooms with a low affective filter and opportunities for students to interact in the target language.

Incorporating Academic Vocabulary

Academic vocabulary must be identified, explicitly taught, and practiced in order to develop fluency in academic language. Academic language is the language used in textbooks, classroom lectures, and assessments. It includes the, "specialized vocabulary, grammar, discourse/textual, and functional skills associated with academic instruction and mastery of academic material and tasks" (Goldenberg & Coleman, 2010). It tends to be more grammatically complex than social language, and it has more content-specific vocabulary. This type of language often poses a formidable task for students, especially ELs.

Academic language is different from the social language EL students use outside of classroom situations. For ELs to be successful in school, they must not only have oral English proficiency, but also a command of academic English because it enables them to be educationally competitive with native English speakers. Being proficient in informal oral language does not necessarily correlate with success in reading for students. To be successful, they must be proficient in formal oral language. For example, significant research shows that ELs who perform well on informal oral language proficiency tests—such as the Basic Inventory of Natural Language—do not necessarily perform well on reading assessments. On the other hand, ELs who perform well on oral proficiency tests with an emphasis on formal academic language—such as the Woodcock Language Proficiency Battery—do tend to perform well on reading assessments (Goldenberg & Coleman, 2010). This shows the vital importance of oral academic language development to teachers of ELs.

It is important to remember, however, that social language development is still significant for ELs. Not all ELs will develop social English before they develop academic English. For example, a student who begins with a high level of proficiency in his/her native academic language may be able to develop an understanding of academic English more rapidly than he/she can adapt to standard social English conventions. Both social and academic English are necessary for success in a school where instruction is in English. Therefore, teachers of ELs should create opportunities within content-area classes in order to develop both.

Many students classified as ELs come from lower socio-economic backgrounds. A variety of studies have demonstrated that these students tend to have less academic vocabulary than their middle-class and upper-class peers (Marzano, 2004). Although many ELs become proficient in oral language within a few years of attending American schools, this oral proficiency does not enable them to master grade-level content or be successful on standardized assessments.

COMPREHENSIBLE OUTPUT is the effective use of English speech in oral and written communication (Swain, 1995). When ELs have low-stress opportunities to talk and write, they are able to practice new language structures and notice gaps in their existing language knowledge. This often prompts them to dialogue with other students and use resources to fill those gaps. In addition, short conversations and writing opportunities provide students a chance to reflect on their language learning and internalize their linguistic knowledge. In a sheltered classroom opportunities for output occur throughout instruction and not simply as a reflection at the end of the lesson.

A command of academic English requires knowledge of different kinds of academic vocabulary. Dutro & Kinsella (2010) identify two types of academic vocabulary as brick or mortar words. Brick words are the core content-area words that are necessary for the mastery of a particular subject. These kinds of words are typically found in the glossary of a content-area textbook or in bold or italicized print throughout the textbook. Mortar words are the academic words that link brick words together; they make content-area text coherent and accessible. Brick words tend to be taught directly and explicitly within content-area classes. Mortar words are not typically taught directly in content-area classes. Instead, teachers of ELs must place a greater emphasis on explaining, modeling, and using mortar words in context to ensure success with these words. Note the chart below with examples of brick and mortar words.

Content-Area Examples	MATH Shapes	SCIENCE Water Cycle	LANGUAGE ARTS Literary Elements	SOCIAL STUDIES Revolutionary War
BRICK Content Obligatory Words	polygon, quadrilateral, parallel, rhombus, rectangle, etc.	cumulus, evaporation, precipitation, condensation, etc.	element, character, plot, setting, problem, solution, etc.	Redcoats, revolution, taxations, patriots, representation, etc.
MORTAR Process Functional Words Content Compatible	**Compare & Contrast Words:** similar different example between therefore	**Sequence Words:** first next finally	**Discussion Words:** agree disagree because opinion possibility however	**Cause and Effect and Discussion Words:** cause effect as a result agree & disagree because opinion possibility however

Promoting Literacy and Language Development

For ELs to excel in school, educators must focus on both language and literacy development. Although literacy and language are related concepts, they have clear distinctions. Understanding the differences between a focus on literacy, as opposed to a focus on language, will help EL educators plan and deliver effective lessons to address both concepts.

Literacy is defined in a variety of ways, and the concept of literacy has evolved significantly. Webster's Dictionary provides two definitions of literacy that are somewhat reflective of current thought. One definition of literacy describes it as the ability to read and write. This is the definition most educators recall when they hear the term literacy. For example, if we hear that a nation has a low literacy rate, we understand that a large number of citizens lack the ability to read and write in the language of that country. Webster's Dictionary also defines literacy as knowledge of a particular subject area. For example, the National Center for Science Education (NCSE, 2013) describes scientific literacy as, "the knowledge and understanding of scientific concepts and processes required for personal decision-making, participation in civic/cultural affairs, and economic productivity."

To understand this definition of literacy, it is helpful to reflect on the question: "What exactly does it mean to be a literate person?" Becoming a literate person involves more than the skill of decoding text and comprehending meaning. Achieving literacy involves developing a broad schema that includes specific knowledge of a variety of subjects, enabling one to communicate in a particular environment. A large part of becoming literate in a school environment means being able to navigate academic content in a particular discipline. Because language is "the primary vehicle for intellectual development," (Echevarria, Vogt, & Short, 2017) literacy and language development are significantly related to one another. The primary focus of literacy development is fostering academically literate students who can navigate a variety of academic subjects, and the goal of language development is to develop fluency in social and academic English.

To better understand language development, it is helpful to reflect on yet another question: "What does it mean to be fluent in a particular language?" Fluency involves more than being able to speak a language. To be fluent in academic English, one must be able to read, write, listen, and speak in a variety of contexts with a variety of goals.

In order to facilitate literacy and language development, teachers of ELs must focus on both in every lesson. This especially holds true for teachers in sheltered classes. Research on EL instruction indicates that an approach focusing on two separate objectives—a content objective and a language

MARZANO (2004) HAS OUTLINED A SIX-STEP PROCESS FOR TEACHING CORE CONTENT TERMS (BRICK WORDS) BASED ON HIS RESEARCH. THEY ARE:

1. The teacher provides a description, explanation, or example of a new term.

2. Students restate the explanation of the new term in their own words.

3. Students create a nonlinguistic representation of the term.

4. Students periodically complete activities that add to their knowledge of terms.

5. Students periodically discuss the terms with one another.

6. Students periodically play vocabulary games with the new terms.

objective –is an effective way to meet these two goals for ELs (Echevarria, Vogt, & Short, 2017; Goldenberg & Coleman, 2010; Castillo, 2012).

Content objectives focus on developing a deep understanding of the content and are aligned to the state standards of any given state and to a particular level of Bloom's taxonomy. Language objectives focus on providing an opportunity for students to acquire targeted language forms and functions (Norris & Ortega, 2000). Language objectives can be aligned to the language proficiency standards of each state and include a specific language process for reading, writing, listening and speaking.

What's the difference between content and language objectives?

Content and language objectives are predetermined expectations that guide lessons and help students focus on specific goals. They explain what students will learn (related to content and language) and define what they will be able to do by the end of each lesson.

Content	Language
· Align with content standards	· Align with ELPS
· Focus on mastery of academic content	· Focus on mastery of English language skills

Here are some real classroom examples:

Kindergarten

5th Grade

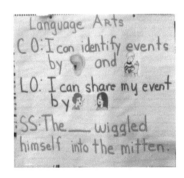

State and district curriculum standards provide a concrete framework for teachers to decide what information to teach (Seidlitz, 2011). Effective content and language objectives are both measurable and observable.

Ask yourself:

- Are my objectives written in student-friendly language?
- Are my objectives posted and visible for all students to see?
- Do I introduce my objectives at the beginning of each lesson?
- Do I close my lesson by going back to the objectives and asking my students if they met the objectives?

Follow the step-by-step process on the next page to write content and language objectives that are observable and measurable.

Content and language objectives must be written and displayed in the language used to deliver the lesson. If the lesson is delivered in Spanish (during the Spanish block of bilingual/ESL instruction), the objective must be written and communicated in Spanish. If the lesson is delivered in English (during the ELD block of bilingual/ESL instruction), the objective must be written and communicated in English.

Content Objective

I will _(verb+TEKS)_ **by/using** _(academic task)_ .
  /   /   /
WHO WHAT   **HOW**

FOR EXAMPLE:
I can identify the water cycle by creating and labeling a diagram.

I can see a student creating a diagram. This makes the objective **OBSERVABLE.**

I can measure whether or not the student identified the parts of the diagram and labeled them correctly. This makes the objective **MEASURABLE.**

Language Objective

I will _(domain/ELPS)_ **by/using** _(specific words, phrases, or stems)_ .
  /   /   /
WHO WHAT   **HOW**

FOR EXAMPLE:
I can discuss with my partner the difference between _____ (condensation, precipitation, evaporation, etc.) and _____ (condensation, precipitation, evaporation, etc.) using:

_____ is the same as . . .

_____ and _____ have . . .

_____ is similar/different than _____ in that . . .

I can see the students talking to one another. This makes the objective **OBSERVABLE.**

I can hear the students using specific words and phrases so they can develop academic language. This makes the objective **MEASURABLE.**

Why do we use both content and language objectives when providing instruction to ELs?

To meet the needs of ELs, a well-designed lesson should focus on the language skills necessary to accomplish literacy tasks. Content objectives are aligned to the TEKS, and language objectives are aligned to the ELPS. The writing of content and language objectives ensures that teachers not only meet state expectations of implementing the standards, but also intentionally support ELs with the development of formal/informal English content and language skills—listening, speaking, reading, and writing in all content areas—while moving ELs to higher levels of language proficiency. Similarly, Spanish language learners (SLLs) in Two-Way Dual Language programs benefit from both content and language objectives as they develop their formal/informal Spanish content and language skills.

How do the ELPS apply to lesson planning for ELs?

The language standards (ELPS) address various levels of proficiency. When planning lessons, it is important to focus not only on developing reading and writing skills, but also listening and speaking skills. The implementation of the ELPS (listening and speaking) ensures that students are able to participate in discussions as they learn new language heard in classroom interactions and understand general meaning, main points, and details. Similarly, as they use new vocabulary in stories, descriptions, and classroom communication and give information using content-area vocabulary, they practice and

familiarize themselves with a variety of grammatical structures. Furthermore, the development of oral language skills (listening and speaking) contributes to the development of literacy skills (reading and writing), including word recognition, grammar, and comprehension.

How do the TEKS apply to lesson planning for ELs?

English learners in bilingual/ESL programs are expected to receive high-quality, rigorous instruction in all content areas to develop literacy and academic skills in the primary language and English. According to Chapter 89 of TAC, the goal of bilingual/ESL education programs is to enable ELs to become competent in listening, speaking, reading, and writing, but also to gain mastery of literacy skills in mathematics, science, and social studies [TAC §89.1201 (b). Policy].

When bilingual/ESL teachers develop lessons for daily instruction, they must use the content standards or TEKS. Instruction, pacing, and materials can be modified to ensure that ELs have a full opportunity to master the required curriculum [TAC §89.1210. Program Content and Design].

> The implementation of the ELPS (listening and speaking) ensures that students are able to participate in discussions as they learn new language heard in classroom interactions and understand general meaning, main points, and details.

Language Objective Stems

LEARNING STRATEGIES

1A: Use what they know about ___ to predict the meaning of ...

1B: Check how well they are able to say ...

1C: Use ___ to learn new vocabulary about...

1D: Use strategies such as ___ to discuss...

1E: Use and reuse the words/phrases ___ in a discussion/writing activity about...

1F: Use the phrase ___ to learn the meaning of ...

1G: Use formal/informal English to describe...

1H: Use strategies such as ___ to learn the meaning of...

LISTENING

2A: Recognize correct pronunciation of....

2B: Recognize sounds used in the words...

2C: Identify words and phrases heard in a discussion about ...

2D: Check for understanding by.... /Seek help by...

2E: Use __ (media source) to learn/review....

2F: Listen to and derive meaning from ___about...

2G: Describe general meaning, main points, and details heard in...

2H: Identify implicit ideas and information heard in ...

2I: Demonstrate listening comprehension by...

SPEAKING

3A: Pronounce the words ___ correctly.

3B: Use new vocabulary about ___ in stories, pictures, descriptions, and/or classroom communication ...

3C: Speak using a variety of types of sentence stems about ...

3D: Speak using the words___ about...

3E: Share in cooperative groups about ...

3F: Ask and give information using the words...

3G: Express opinions, ideas, and feelings about ___ using the words/phrases...

3H: Narrate, describe, and explain....

3I: Use formal/informal English to say ...

3J: Respond orally to information from a variety of media sources about...

READING

4A: Identify relationships between sounds and letters by...

4B: Recognize directionality of English text.

4C: Recognize the words/phrases...

4D: Use prereading supports such as___ to understand...

4E: Read materials about ___ with support of simplified text/visuals/word banks as needed.

4F: Use visual and contextual supports to read...

4G: Show comprehension of English text about...

4H: Demonstrate comprehension of text read silently by...

4I: Show comprehension of text about ___ through basic reading skills such as ...

4J: Show comprehension of text/graphic sources about ___ through inferential skills such as...

4K: Show comprehension of text about ___ through analytical skills such as...

WRITING

5A: Learn relationships between sounds and letters when writing about ...

5B: Write using newly-acquired vocabulary about...

5C: Spell English words such as ...

5D: Edit writing about ...

5E: Use simple and complex sentences to write about ...

5F: Write using a variety of sentence frames and selected vocabulary about ...

5G: Narrate, describe, and explain in writing about...

Scaffolding for All Language Levels

It is essential for teachers of ELs to scaffold instruction. In doing so, they provide student support that leads to independence. In the context of language development, scaffolding provides specific targeted support so that students gradually become self-sufficient in their language production.

Oral scaffolding is the use of oral language that includes teacher modeling and support. Examples of oral scaffolding include recasting (repeating a student's response with correct English structures), rephrasing student responses, paraphrasing, and providing appropriate wait time. When providing oral scaffolding to students, it is unnecessary to have students repeat responses once they are recasted, paraphrased, or rephrased.

Procedural scaffolding gradually increases the level of EL independence (Fisher & Frey, 2007). Teachers provide procedural scaffolding through three sequential processes: I do, We do, You do.

When scaffolding language development, it is helpful to think of the three phases as "I use the language, we use the language, you use the language." First, the teacher models language use. Then, the teacher uses choral response or shared writing to use language with the students. Finally, the students speak or write independently.

Instructional scaffolding is the third type of scaffolding and includes support for language output. Instructional scaffolding facilitates independent use and access to the English language by explicitly teaching linguistic structures and strategies. Examples of instructional scaffolding include paragraph frames, think-alouds, and graphic organizers, which provide processes to organize thinking in order to produce language.

The SIOP model identifies three ways teachers can scaffold instruction for ELs (Echevarria, Vogt, & Short, 2017):

ORAL
SCAFFOLDING

PROCEDURAL
SCAFFOLDING

INSTRUCTIONAL
SCAFFOLDING

	DEFINITIONS & EXAMPLES
Oral Scaffolding	• Recasting • Rephrasing • Paraphrasing • Providing appropriate wait time • Sentence Frames
Procedural Scaffolding	• Moving from whole class, to partner to individual language use. • I do…, we do…, you do…
Instructional Scaffolding	• Paragraph frames • Graphic organizers • Think-alouds • Genre analysis

Math Stem Wall

One thing I remember about _____ is …

The solution is probably …

My estimate is correct because …

_____ is reasonable because …

One example might be …

Content Objective:
Students will demonstrate application of graphing and displaying data by sketching circle graphs using information gathered from a survey.

Language Objective:
Students will write about their graphs using the words circle graph, data, percent, etc.
Stems:
My circle graph shows…
The data…
My information…
What I concluded is _____, because….

Agenda:
- Finish soft drink surveys
- Complete favorite sport surveys
- Work in groups to create bar and circle graphs
- Complete Venn diagrams

Bar Graph   Circle Graph

Word Wall

solution   equation
estimate   similar
reasonable   table
function   origin
data   integer
variable   predict
percentage

6. THE 7 STEPS TO A LANGUAGE-RICH, INTERACTIVE CLASSROOM

7-STEPS:

1 Teach Students What to Say When They Don't Know What to Say

2 Have Students Speak in Complete Sentences

3 Randomize and Rotate When Calling on Students

4 Use Total Response Signals

5 Use Targeted Visual and Vocabulary Strategies

6 Have Students Participate in Structured Conversations

7 Have Students Participate in Structured Reading and Writing Activities

Step 1: Teach Students What to Say When They Don't Know What to Say

As teachers who work with diverse students, such as ELs, one of the biggest challenges facing us is the phenomenon known as learned helplessness. It seems that as parents and teachers, we actually train students to be helpless. Every time we ask students to respond to a question or perform a task and fail to hold them accountable for their response or performance, we send them a message: You are not expected to achieve. By teaching students how to help themselves, we enable them to overcome learned helplessness and really become independent learners. It is not enough just to tell students to think for themselves and to try harder. We have to teach many of our students, especially ELs, the language and habits of independent learners so that they can become independent learners. Teaching our students how to acquire helpful information when they are confused and teaching them to think about the steps involved in reaching a specific goal gives them skills they can use inside and outside of school. Imagine that a principal asks a group of 3rd grade teachers to gather specific data on students from various subpopulations. The teachers look at the request and discover they don't know how to find information on the students. As a result, they write on the form, "We don't know," and put it in the principal's box. How do you think the principal would react? In the professional world, such behavior would never be acceptable. Yet, as teachers, we have all been frustrated by calling on students who maintain a long silence as they stare at the floor, shrug their shoulders, and say, "I don't know." We are all looking for ways to banish, "I don't know," "Huh," and "What," from our classrooms. One solution that works is to teach students to respond differently when they are unsure about an answer for a question. There are specific alternatives that help students get past the "I don't know" stage. This creates an expectation of accountable conversation.

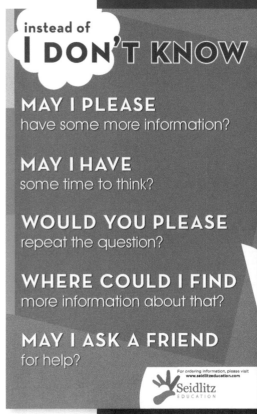

instead of
I DON'T KNOW

MAY I PLEASE have some more information?

MAY I HAVE some time to think?

WOULD YOU PLEASE repeat the question?

WHERE COULD I FIND more information about that?

MAY I ASK A FRIEND for help?

For ordering information, please visit
www.seidlitzeducation.com
Seidlitz EDUCATION

On the first or second day of school, demonstrate how to use the responses and explain the procedure. Subsequently, all students are responsible for participating. After modeling the way to use the responses, explain what is meant by the expectation of accountable conversation. Whenever a teacher asks a question, students have two choices: respond to the teacher or request assistance and then respond. The important principle is that students must always respond. They might not respond correctly and they might need some extra time or support, but opting out of the conversation is not an option.

After initially introducing the expectation of accountable conversation to students and using the poster of alternative responses in the classroom, we are ready to branch out and teach students what to say when they don't know what to say in other ways. In a science class, we might train students to ask for help and clarification during a lab. For example, "What is my job during this step?" In a language arts class, we could teach students how to ask each other questions when working in literature circles when they don't understand the conversation in the group. For example, "Could you please try to explain that in a different way?" Additionally, we could train kindergarten students to say, "Can you tell me how to_____?" when they need help in the lunch room, on the playground, or on the way to the bus. The basic idea is to give students specific sentences and questions to use in different situations so that they can independently seek help when they need it.

THE RESEARCH

TEACH STUDENTS WHAT TO SAY WHEN THEY DON'T KNOW WHAT TO SAY

Teaching students what to say when they don't know what to say is a metacognitive strategy.

It teaches students to monitor their own thinking to determine whether or not they understand, and it helps them make thoughtful choices so they can access help and support for their learning. The use of metacognitive strategies has an impact on student learning **(Duffy, 2002; McLaughlin, 2003; Snow, Griffin, & Burns, 2005)**. Research on language learners and learning strategies concludes that all learners, including English learners, benefit from learning when they use metacognitive strategies to monitor and evaluate their own thinking **(Chamot, 2004).** English learners need to explore different learning strategies, experiment with them, and evaluate them. By doing this, students are able to choose their own effective strategies.

Teachers must consider the connection between language levels and learner strategies. Students at higher levels of proficiency demonstrate more confidence in using strategies similar to their English speaking counterparts. However, students at the beginning levels of language proficiency often do not have enough English language L2 proficiency to understand why and how to use specific learning strategies. When possible, teachers should use the student's primary language (L1) to explain the new learning strategies. Teachers must explicitly teach a new strategy in simple academic language, model the strategy, allow students to use it, and provide students time for self-reflection. The use of appropriate learning strategies allows students to take responsibility for their learning by enhancing autonomy, independence, and self-direction **(Oxford & Nyikos, 1989)**.

Step 2: Have Students Speak in Complete Sentences

In Step 2, the development of high levels of English oral language proficiency is the priority. Academic success in the United States requires proficiency in oral English (Goldenberg & Coleman, 2010). Consequently, students must go beyond knowing vocabulary words; they must learn how to form and structure these words in the academic language they read, write, and speak. They need to know how to express complex meanings orally even if they are limited in English language proficiency. Teachers must remember that students have trouble writing in ways they cannot speak. The expectation and preparation of students to respond in complete sentences allows them to participate in learning in a formal way. Although expectations must be appropriate for their language level, ELs will perform better if there are set expectations based on academic achievement rather than solely on language proficiency levels. Second language research suggests the need to pay attention to both second language acquisition and language form (Schmidt, 2010). Having students share and respond to both the teacher and other students using complete sentences with specific grammatical structures can be a successful integrated approach to teaching ELs the forms and meanings of English. Similarly, it facilitates the opportunity to assess both language and literacy development.

EIGHTH GRADE CLASSROOM A	EIGHTH GRADE CLASSROOM B
Teacher: Okay, class, yesterday we discussed the three branches of government. Let's see if we can remember what those are. Sonia, can you tell us the three branches of government?	Teacher: Okay, class, yesterday we discussed the three branches of government. Let's see if we can remember what those are. Sonia, can you tell us the three branches of government?
Sonia: Executive, legislative, and the one with the judges.	Sonia: The three branches of government are the executive branch, the legislative branch, and the one with the judges.
Teacher: Judicial, that's right. What is the judicial branch responsible for doing?	Teacher: The judicial branch, that's right. What is the judicial branch responsible for doing?
Sonia: The court cases.	Sonia: I think the judicial branch is responsible for, um, mostly listening to cases in court and deciding who is right and wrong.
Teacher: Good. Everyone take out your homework and find question 3, which asks about the judicial branch. Joey, what did you select?	Teacher: Good. Everyone take out your homework and find question 3, which asks about the judicial branch. Joey, what did you select?
Joey: Umm, for number 3? Uh, C.	Joey: Umm for number 3? Uh... the responsibilities of the judicial branch include (C). interpreting the Constitution and deciding cases.
Teacher: That's right. The responsibilities of the judicial branch include (C). interpreting the Constitution and deciding cases.	Teacher: That's right.

FIFTH GRADE CLASSROOM A	FIFTH GRADE CLASSROOM B
Teacher: Okay class, yesterday we talked about all the different parts of a story. We called them literary elements. Sonia, can you remember one of the literary elements we talked about?	Teacher: Okay class, yesterday we talked about all the different parts of a story. We called them literary elements. Sonia, can you remember one of the literary elements we talked about?
Sonia: Problem.	Sonia: One of the literary elements is the problem.
Teacher: The problem. That is one of the literary elements. What is the problem in a story?	Teacher: The problem is one of the literary elements. What is the problem in a story?
Sonia: The bad part.	Sonia: It is the bad part in the story.
Teacher: Tell me more.	Teacher: Tell me more.
Sonia: Like fixing the wrong part.	Sonia: It's like fixing the wrong part. The problem has to get fixed.
Teacher: Okay. Good. Joey, what is another literary element we discussed yesterday?	Teacher: Okay. Good. Joey, what is another literary element we discussed yesterday?
Joey: Umm...	Joey: Umm...
Teacher: What is another important part of every story?	Teacher: What is another important part of every story?
Joey: People, umm, the characters.	Joey: Another important part is the people, umm, the characters.
	Teacher: That's right.

In classroom A, there is no expectation for students to use complete sentences; whereas, in classroom B, there is. It is clear in both conversations that Sonia and Joey have some content understanding. However, it is only in classroom B that their communication reflects their social studies and language arts class content.

This simple expectation dramatically improves the quality of interactions in our classroom. When we encourage our students to use complete sentences, they think in complete thoughts. They link new words to new concepts and are able to practice using academic language structures.

Picture, for a moment, a student named Natalie. She is an 8th grader in a U.S. history class. The teacher calls on Natalie and asks her to explain what the class just read. Natalie thinks for a moment and then says, *Ok now, there were the British ones...and the other ones and they didn't like each other, with the taxation representation thingy...and they were all throwing tea into the water and were mad and stuff and wanted you know...independence and everything. They called it a tea party, but they didn't have no balloons or nothing.* Any 8th grade teacher knows that this kind of response is all too common. Predictably, when Natalie writes her thoughts on paper, she will write exactly the same way. She simply does not know how to communicate using formal academic language.

It's very hard for students to write in a way they cannot speak. By providing students with opportunities to communicate, we give them the gift of academic language and a passport to communicate in the professional world. The beginning of the process is learning to communicate our thoughts completely by using complete sentences. Not every single interaction in the classroom between the teacher and the students, and among students, requires complete sentences. Sometimes, informal language is appropriate, even in professional settings. However, students must be given experience in using formal language. It is very important to provide ample opportunities in class that require students to use complete sentences in oral communication. In doing so, students learn how to develop their thoughts and use formal language structures.

One way to support students as they learn to respond with complete sentences is to provide them with a sentence stem. A sentence stem is a short phrase that gives students the beginning of a sentence and helps them structure a response. Using sentence stems dramatically changes the quality and tone of a classroom because it helps students become increasingly more comfortable using academic language for expression.

> BY PROVIDING STUDENTS WITH OPPORTUNITIES TO COMMUNICATE, WE GIVE THEM THE GIFT OF ACADEMIC LANGUAGE AND A PASSPORT TO COMMUNICATE IN THE PROFESSIONAL WORLD.

How do I support students when they struggle with the use of complete sentences?

Sometimes students do not speak in complete sentences because they do not have the confidence, opportunities to practice, or sufficient English proficiency to do so. In order to enable students to speak in complete sentences, sometimes we need to provide support that helps them to be successful with this skill independently. Nancy Motley, author of *Talk, Read, Talk, Write* (2016), provides 3 steps to help when scaffolding complete sentences:

1. Let students talk more! If the only opportunity students are getting to practice is the one or two times they are called on by the teacher, they are not receiving enough practice. Students need many opportunities for output throughout each lesson. Incorporating more partner talk and group collaboration will help increase each student's opportunity to speak.

2. Tweak their talk. Each time students are asked to share (turn and talk; think, pair, share; group discussion, etc.), the teacher should identify clear goals for student conversations. Some great phrases for this include: "I'm listening for…," "It should sound like this…," "Here's your sentence stem…"

3. Coach for it! Some students will need a lot of linguistic support while others may only need a visual cue to remind them to form a complete sentence. When a student responds with one word or a short phrase, here are **4 strategies for "coaching" students to use complete sentences** (ranging from most support to least support):

Choral Response – The teacher puts the student response in a complete sentence and asks the class to repeat it.

Sentence Stem – The teacher provides the first half of the response and the student repeats that part and completes the response.

Key Word or Phrase – The teacher provides a key word or phrase that the student should include in their response.

Gesture – The teacher provides a non-verbal gesture to cue the student to rephrase their response in a complete sentence (e.g., nodding while using both hands to demonstrate "stretching" an imaginary rubber band).

Each student will need a different level of linguistic support, so it is important that the teacher differentiates based upon what he or she knows about each student's proficiency. Some students will need choral response for many months while others might only need coaching with a keyword or phrase a few times before they are able to independently form complete sentences.

Sentence Frames - Varying Thinking Stems

lead4ward · Seidlitz EDUCATION

Analyze & Interpret

		Cognate
BEGINNING	_____ occurs more/less frequently than _____.	ocurre, con más/menos frequencia
	_____ is/is not important because _____.	es/no es importante
INTERMEDIATE	The information from _____ tells me that _____.	información, informe
	Based upon _____, I believe_____ is more/less important than _____.	basado/ a en, es más/menos importante
ADVANCED	After a careful analysis of _____ I can state with certainty that _____.	análisis, con certeza
	I analyze/interpret the information to mean_____ due to _____.	información, interpreto, analizo

Apply

		Cognate
BEGINNING	_____ is an example of _____.	ejemplo
	I use _____ when I _____.	uso
INTERMEDIATE	I used _____ to determine that _____.	determinar
	When I solve this problem, I need to know _____ and _____.	problema
ADVANCED	A possible result of _____ is _____.	posible, resultado
	_____ is another instance where this applies.	instancia, aplica

Cause & Effect

		Cognate
BEGINNING	The cause of _____ is/ was _____ because _____.	causa
	The effect of _____ is/was _____ because _____.	efecto
INTERMEDIATE	There are/were many causes for _____ including _____.	causas incluyendo
	There are/were many effects of _____ including _____.	efectos incluyendo
ADVANCED	The cause(s) of _____ was/were _____, and the effect(s) was/were _____.	causas efectos
	The most significant cause of ____ is/was ____ and the most significant effect is/was ____.	causa significativa/efecto significativo

Compare Classify & Categorize

		Cognate
BEGINNING	_____ is similar to/different from _____ because _____.	similar, diferente
	The difference between _____ and _____ is _____.	diferencia
INTERMEDIATE	The characteristics of _____ are similar to/different from _____.	caracteristicas, similares
	One distinction between _____ and _____ is _____.	distinción entre
ADVANCED	While _____ and _____ are similar, _____ is distinct.	similar, distinto
	In this circumstance, it is clear that _____ and _____ are comparable.	en esta circunstancia, está claro que, comparable

beginning --> advanced

Sentence Frames - Varying Thinking Stems

lead4ward   Seidlitz EDUCATION

Create Develop

Cognate

BEGINNING

I can create _____ with _____.   crear

I would use _____ to _____.   usaría

INTERMEDIATE

I could demonstrate this by_____.   mostrar

A different way to design_____ is _____.   diferente, diseñar

ADVANCED

With what I know, I could create a _____.   crear

The way I would explain this to another kid is _____.   explicar

Draw Conclusions

Cognate

BEGINNING

I conclude _____ is correct/incorrect because _____.   concluyo, correcto/incorrecto

I imagined _____, but now I think _____.   imaginé

INTERMEDIATE

One conclusion I can make is _____ because _____.   conclusión

With this new information, I can now state _____.   información

ADVANCED

Based on my reflection, I conclude _____ because _____.   Basado en, la reflexión, concluyo

_____ is significant/reasonable in this case because _____.   significativo, en este caso, razonamiento

Evaluate

Cognate

BEGINNING

It is my opinion that _____ is a good/bad idea because_____.   opinión, idea

My evaluation is that _____ is important because _____.   evaluación, importante

INTERMEDIATE

In my opinion, I believe that _____ because_____.   opinión

The importance of _____ is _____.   importancia

ADVANCED

As my evaluation of _____ concluded it is evident that _____.   evaluación, concluido, evidente

After careful analysis, I can say that _____ has value because _____.   análisis, tiene valor

Generalize

Cognate

BEGINNING

While there are exceptions, I can generally say this information tells us that _____.   generalmente

Frequently_____ is/are _____ because they are/it has_____.   frecuentemente

INTERMEDIATE

According to [the text/information], you can generally say _____.   De acuerdo con el [texto, información], generalmente

Most of the time _____. I believe that because _____.

ADVANCED

You can generally say the more/less_____, the more/less _____.   generalmente

I believe, based upon _____, that generally _____.   basado/ a en, generalmente

beginning --> advanced

Sentence Frames - Varying Thinking Stems

lead4ward **Seidlitz** EDUCATION

Infer

Cognate

BEGINNING

The book/text says _____, so I think _____.
texto

It appears that _____ because _____.
aparece

INTERMEDIATE

One piece of evidence that informs my decision is _____.
La evidencia que, informa, decisión

The text stated _____, which is why I think _____.
texto

ADVANCED

Although not explicitly stated, I can infer _____ because _____.
explícitamente, puedo inferir

The evidence indicates _____ because _____.
evidencia, indica

Make Connections

Cognate

BEGINNING

This reminds me of _____.

Another example of _____ is _____.
otro, ejemplo

INTERMEDIATE

_____ is similar to this because _____.
similar

_____ reminds me of _____.

ADVANCED

The main connection between _____ and _____ is _____.
conexión/relación

_____ and _____ are related in at least two ways, _____ and _____.
relacionados

Predict Estimate

Cognate

BEGINNING

I predict/estimate _____ because _____ is/are _____.
predigo

I think _____ will repeat because _____ is/are _____.
repito

INTERMEDIATE

I predict/estimate _____. My reasons for this include _____.
predigo , las razones, incluyen

In my opinion, _____ will happen next because _____.
en mi opinión

ADVANCED

In light of _____, I predict _____.
predigo

In consideration of the text/information given, I believe _____ will occur.
en consideración a/al, texto, información

Sequence / Order

Cognate

BEGINNING

_____ happened before/after _____.

The order of events begins/terminates with _____.
orden de eventos, termina

INTERMEDIATE

A vital step in the process is _____ because _____.
vital, proceso

Considering _____, it is not a surprise that _____ occurred.
considerando que, sorpresa, occurió

ADVANCED

It would be important to _____ before/after _____.
importante

If all the steps are complete, _____ will occur.
completos, ocurrirá

beginning --> advanced

Sentence Frames - Varying Thinking Stems

lead4ward | Seidlitz EDUCATION

Summarize

		Cognate
BEGINNING	It's important to remember _____.	importante
	Three important points, ideas, or actions are _____.	tres, ideas importantes, acciones
INTERMEDIATE	It is essential to know _____.	esencial
	The most important part is _____ because _____.	parte más importante
ADVANCED	After _____, I now understand _____.	
	The most significant thing I learned today is _____.	significante

beginning --> advanced

Sentence Frames - Varying Thinking Stems

lead4ward **Seidlitz EDUCATION**

Analizar e Interpretar

Cognado

BEGINNING

_____ ocurre con más/menos frecuencia que _____. occurs more/less frequently than

_____ es/no es importante porque _____. is/is not important

INTERMEDIATE

La información de _____ me dice que _____. information

Basado/a en _____, yo creo que_____ es más/menos importante que _____. based upon, is more/less important than

ADVANCED

Después de un cuidadoso análisis de _____ puedo decir con certeza que _____. analysis of, with certainty

Yo analizo/interpreto la información en el sentido de _____ debido a _____. analyze/interpret the information

Aplicar

Cognado

BEGINNING

_____ es un ejemplo de _____. example

Yo uso _____ cuando yo _____. use

INTERMEDIATE

Yo usé _____ para determinar que _____. use, to determine

Cuando resuelvo este problema, necesito saber _____ y _____. resolve, problem

ADVANCED

Un posible resultado de _____ es _____. possible result,

_____ es otra instancia donde esto se aplica. instance, applies

Causa y Efecto

Cognado

BEGINNING

La causa de _____ es/era _____ porque _____. cause

El efecto de _____ es/era _____ porque _____. effect

INTERMEDIATE

Hay/Había muchas causas para _____ incluyendo _____. causes, including

Hay/Había muchas efectos para _____ incluyendo _____. effects, including

ADVANCED

La(s) causa(s) de _____ era/eran _____, y el(los) efecto(s) era/eran _____. cause(s), effect(s)

La causa más significativa de _____ es/era _____ el efecto más significativo es/era _____. significant cause, significant effect

Comparar, Clasificar y Categorizar

Cognado

BEGINNING

_____ es similar a/diferente de _____ porque _____. similar to/different from

La diferencia entre _____ y _____ es _____. difference

INTERMEDIATE

Las características de _____ son similares a/diferentes de _____. characteristics, similar/different

Una distinción entre _____ y _____ es _____. distinction between

ADVANCED

Mientras que _____ y _____ son similares, _____ es distinto. similar, distinct

En esta circunstancia, está claro que _____ y _____ son comparables. in this circumstance, it is clear that, comparable

beginning --> advanced

Sentence Frames - Varying Thinking Stems

lead4ward · Seidlitz EDUCATION

Crear, Desarrollar

Cognado

BEGINNING

Yo puedo crear _____ con _____ . create

Yo usaría _____ para _____ . would use

INTERMEDIATE

Yo podría demostrar esto al _____ . demonstrate

Una manera diferente de diseñar _____ es _____ . different, design

ADVANCED

Con lo que sé, yo podría crear _____ . create

La manera en la que voy a explicar esto a otro estudiante _____ . explain, student

Sacar Conclusiones

Cognado

BEGINNING

Yo concluyo que _____ es correcto/incorrecto porque _____ . conclude, correct/incorrect

Yo imaginé que _____, pero ahora pienso que _____ . imagined

INTERMEDIATE

Una conclusión que puedo hacer es que _____ porque _____ . conclusion

Con esta nueva información, ahora puedo afirmar que _____ . information

ADVANCED

Basado(a) en mi reflexión, concluyo _____ porque _____ . based on my reflection, I conclude

_____ es significativo/razonable en este caso porque _____ . is significant/reasonable in this case

Evaluar

Cognado

BEGINNING

Es mi opinión que _____ es una buena/mala idea porque _____ . opinion, idea

Mi evaluación es que _____ es importante porque _____ . evaluation, important

INTERMEDIATE

En mi opinión, yo creo que _____ porque _____ . opinion

La importancia de _____ es _____ . importance

ADVANCED

Como concluyó mi evaluación de _____ es evidente que _____ . concluded, evaluation, evident

Después de un análisis cuidadoso, puedo decir que _____ tiene valor porque _____ . analysis, has value

Generalizar

Cognado

BEGINNING

Aunque hay excepciones, generalmente puedo decir que esta información nos dice que ___. exceptions, generally, information

Frecuentemente _____ es/son _____ porque [es(son)/tiene(n)] _____ . frequently

INTERMEDIATE

De acuerdo con [el texto/la información], generalmente se puede decir que _____ . according to [the text / information], generally

La mayor parte del tiempo, _____. Lo creo porque _____ . time

ADVANCED

Generalmente puedes decir que cuanto más/menos _____, más/menos _____ . generally

Creo, basado/a en _____, que generalmente _____ . based upon, generally

beginning --> advanced

Sentence Frames - Varying Thinking Stems

lead4ward · Seidlitz EDUCATION

Inferir

		Cognado
BEGINNING	El libro/texto dice que _____, por eso yo pienso que _____.	text
	Parece que _____ porque _____.	appears
INTERMEDIATE	Una pieza de evidencia que informa mi decisión es _____.	piece of evidence that, informs, decision
	El texto afirma que _____, por lo que pienso que _____.	text
ADVANCED	Aunque no ha sido afirmado explícitamente, puedo inferir _____ porque _____.	explicitly, I can infer
	La evidencia indica _____ porque _____.	evidence indicates

Hacer Conexiones

		Cognado
BEGINNING	Esto me recuerda que _____.	reminds
	Otro ejemplo de _____ es _____.	another example
INTERMEDIATE	_____ es similar a esto porque _____.	similar
	_____ me recuerda a _____.	reminds
ADVANCED	La conexión principal entre _____ y _____ es _____.	connection
	_____ y _____ se relacionan al menos de dos maneras, _____ y _____.	related

Predecir, Estimar

		Cognado
BEGINNING	Yo predigo/estimo que _____ porque _____ es(son)/está(n) _____.	predict/estimate
	Yo pienso que _____ se repetirá porque _____ es(son)/está(n) _____.	repeat
INTERMEDIATE	Yo predigo/estimo que _____. Mis razones para esto incluyen _____.	predict/estimate, reasons, include
	En mi opinión, _____ ocurrirá después porque _____.	in my opinion, will occur
ADVANCED	A la luz de _____, predigo que _____.	predict
	En consideración a(l) texto/la información dada yo creo que _____ ocurrirá.	in consideration of the text / information, occur

Secuencia/Orden

		Cognado
BEGINNING	_____ ocurrió antes/después de _____.	occurred before/after
	El orden de los eventos empieza/termina con _____.	order of events, terminates
INTERMEDIATE	Un paso vital en el proceso es _____ porque _____.	vital, process
	Considerando que _____, no es una sorpresa que _____ ocurriera.	considering, surprise, occurred
ADVANCED	Sería importante _____ antes/después de _____.	important
	Si todos los pasos están completos, _____ ocurrirá.	complete, occur

beginning --> advanced

Sentence Frames - Varying Thinking Stems

lead4ward   Seidlitz EDUCATION

Resumir

BEGINNING

	Cognado
Es importante recordar _____.	important
Tres puntos, ideas o acciones importantes son _____.	Three, ideas, actions, important

INTERMEDIATE

Es esencial saber que _____.	essential
La parte más importante es _____ porque _____.	most important part

ADVANCED

Después de _____, ahora entiendo _____.	understand
Lo más significativo que aprendí hoy es _____.	significant

beginning --> advanced

THE RESEARCH

HAVE STUDENTS SPEAK IN COMPLETE SENTENCES

Developing high levels of English oral proficiency in ELs should be a priority for their teachers, as academic success in the United States requires proficiency in oral English **(Goldenberg & Coleman, 2010)**. Students must go beyond developing vocabulary terms and learn how to form and structure academic language. They need to understand forms and meaning in written language and how to express complex meanings orally even if they are limited in English language proficiency **(NCTE, 2008)**. Teachers must remember that students cannot write in ways they do not speak. The expectation and preparation of students to respond in complete sentences allows them to participate in learning in a formal way. Although it must be appropriate for their language level, students, including language learners, will perform better if there are set expectations based on academic achievement rather than solely on language proficiency levels. Research on second language acquisition suggests the need to pay attention to both second language acquisition and language form **(Schmidt, 2001)**. When students share and respond to the teacher and other students with complete sentences and specific grammatical structures, they are involved in a successful integrated approach that will teach them form and meaning of the English language. Similarly, it facilitates the opportunity to assess both language and literacy development.

Step 3: Randomize and Rotate When Calling on Students

Many teachers have struggled with finding ways to manage a classroom full of diverse learners. The same few students always raise their hands to respond as the rest of the class sits. We often end up calling on the energetic participators because they usually know the answer, and it allows us to maintain the pace of our lesson. Every so often we insist that other students respond, and we are met with frustration, anxiety, or a blank stare.

Solution 1: Randomizing

Randomizing is one effective way to overcome this problem. It requires very little planning. We create a simple system, like using index cards or Popsicle™ sticks with each student's name, and rely on that system when we call on students. This changes the way we ask questions. We avoid using phrases like: "Who can tell me…?" "Let's see who knows…," "Does anyone know…?" and "Can someone tell the class…?" For the most part, these phrases encourage the participatory students who continue to shout out and dominate the discussion. Our goal is to have everyone involved in discussions so that we can assess all students' understanding of concepts, not just those students who enjoy participating. When we do not use random selection to assess students, we are only checking the understanding of a few highly motivated students. When randomizing, the questioning technique then looks like this:

1. Ask the question.

2. Pause.

3. Select a student to respond using a random selection system.

It's important to ask questions without the solicitation of volunteers. In some cases, it actually helps to explicitly ask students not to raise hands; this eliminates the temptation to call only on those who volunteer. Pausing after the question gives everyone a chance to think, and it creates some positive tension as students wonder who will be chosen. Next, we use random selection by drawing an index card from a pile, for example. This ensures that all students are paying attention and have a fair chance to be called on to respond. Asking questions in this way promotes higher student engagement and more accurate assessment of student understanding. With this method, students grow accustomed to always being prepared to respond, and we grow accustomed to using cards or sticks whenever we ask questions or have discussions.

There are three ways to prepare for random selection: wait time, sentence stems, and peer rehearsal.

- Wait time gives students a minute to think about the question and to formulate a response. While reflection is important to most students, ELs need more time to process both the content and the language before each classroom interaction.

- Sentence stems allow students the comfort and the chance to prepare their responses. Sentence stems lower the amount of language students must produce on their own without lowering the cognitive demand of answering the question.

- Peer rehearsal gives students time to share responses with a partner before offering thoughts to the larger group. In addition, students can use this time to get feedback from a peer and to adjust responses as needed.

Solution 2: Rotating

Using a rotation strategy works best with some classroom discussions. Spencer Kagan's Numbered Heads Together (1992) is an easy way to get everyone involved and avoid the problems of calling on the same students again and again.

Here are the steps.

1. Divide students into groups of four.

2. Ask students to count off within the group (1—4) so each person has a number.

3. Ask a question.

4. Give groups a chance to talk to each other about the answer.

5. Ask one number to stand up in each group. For example, "All Ones, please stand."

6. Have the number One person report for the group.

7. Instruct students to respond with this sentence stem if they have the same response as another group: "We agree that _____ because..."

Repeat the procedure with other questions until each number from 1–4 has been called, giving every person an opportunity to speak for their group. Numbered Heads Together is used best with open-ended questions that have more than one possible response. Of course, all students should share their answers in complete sentences. Some other ways to randomize and rotate include: marking a seating chart as students are called on, numbering desks, and using computer programs to randomly select student names. The important thing is not which system we use, but that we have a system in place. It is important to include everyone. Without a system, total participation is impossible. There are times when it may be helpful to have an open dialogue without using index cards or seating charts. Similarly, teachers may like the energy of students calling out answers and freely exchanging ideas. These discussions can be positive experiences for students, but rarely for all students. If we do not have a system in place, there are students being left out. Those students are usually the at-risk pupils, students with special needs, and ELs, all of whom would most benefit from active participation.

Use index cards:
Record each student's name on an index card. Draw one of the index cards from the stack, and ask that student to respond to a given question.

Organize Numbered Heads Together:
Place students in groups of 4 or 5. Have each group member number off from 1–5, explaining that the number they used in the count off will be their number for the remainder of the day. Ask a question, and then randomly select one of the numbers. All students who have that number respond (Kagan, 1992).

Hold a deck of cards:
Hand out one card to each student, then randomize by calling any of the following: red, black, spades, hearts, diamonds, clubs, face cards, certain numbers, etc.

Designate categories:
Assign a category to individual students or tables of students, such as: parts of speech, days of the week, names of planets, or names of historical figures, etc.

Place colored stickers on desks: Place an assortment of colored stickers randomly on student desks. Ask all the reds, yellows, blues, or greens to respond to questions.

Use individual characteristics:
Provide a starting point for randomizing and rotating, such as personal characteristics like hair color, type of shoes, or color of shirt for students to respond to questions.

Scan the class roster or grade book: Choose students at random from the list in the class roster or grade book.

THE RESEARCH

RANDOMIZE AND ROTATE WHEN CALLING ON STUDENTS

Student engagement is highly correlated with student success. However, engaging ELs becomes a challenge when teachers need to accommodate to various levels of language proficiency. Randomizing and rotating student response is an important strategy to maintain a structure of accountability.

This practice supports all students by providing them with additional time to process information, and it gives teachers the opportunity to provide wait time after questioning. Teachers who work closely with ELs need to devote time to the implementation of these strategies and hold all students accountable. Student participation is also important for meaningful learning.

Research suggests that a high level of student participation in classroom discussions results in higher levels of student achievement. Students need to find their own voices and verbally express their interpretation of course content **(Morgenstern, 1992; Hauser, 1990)**. The same holds true for ELs. Research shows that content-based tasks that help students notice, retrieve, and generate language are effective in facilitating second language acquisition **(Long, 1996, 2007)**. Research also indicates that skilled questioning techniques can foster thoughtful and reflective learning leading to higher levels of academic achievement **(Gall, 1984; Dean, 1986)**.

Step 4: Use Total Response Signals

Total response signals are cues students can use to indicate they are ready to respond to a question or ready to move on to new material. Total response signals give ELs the opportunity to demonstrate content-area literacy without having fully developed proficiency in English.

Response signals allow students to prepare for oral or written participation in a non-threatening way, and they provide a very effective tool for gauging student understanding in real time. There are three elements of an effective total response signal.

Total: Total response signals include every student in the classroom: at risk pupils, ELs, students with special needs, gifted students, oppositionally defiant students, and students with interrupted formal education. Total means everyone. **Response:** Every student will make a choice. After questions are posed, students are given an opportunity to make a decision. Students think through what they know to make choices. **Signal:** Once students have responded or made decisions, they will give a response with a visual signal. The signal must be clear enough so that we can immediately survey how many students can respond to the question or decision. Total response signals enable us to consistently check for student understanding. We think of them as instant ongoing assessments used throughout a lesson. With response signals, we don't have to wait for the quiz, test, worksheet, or writing assignment to find out how well our students understand a topic. We can immediately check for understanding and see who is ready to move on and who still needs help. There are four basic types of response signals:

Written Response: Students write their responses on paper, sticky notes, cards, white boards, or chalk boards and hold them up so they are visible to the teacher.

Ready Response: Students show they have finished a task or are ready to begin a new task. For example, the Thinker's Chin means that students keep their hands on their chins until they finish thinking and are ready to respond to a question. When the hand is removed from the chin, they are ready.

Making Choices: Students show their response to a specific set of choices using a physical object or signal. For example, give students letter cards, labeled A, B, C, and D when reviewing a multiple choice test. After reading a question, ask students to show their choice. We can instantly see how students respond to each question.

Ranking: Students show their relative agreement and disagreement with particular statements. For example, ask students if they agree or disagree with the following statement, "We should make a table before setting up an equation to solve this problem." Have students hold up a five to signal agreement and a one to signal disagreement. Ask students who are undecided to hold up a two, three, or four. Ask students to be ready to explain their reasoning.

Written Response	• Hold up Paper	**Making Choices**	• Open Hand/Closed Hand
	• White Boards		• Thumbs Up/Thumbs Down
	• Personal Chalk Boards		• Pens Up/Pens Down
	• Answers on Cards		• Number Wheels
Ready Response	• Hands Up When Ready		• Green Card/Red Card
	• Hands Down When Ready		• Move to the Corner/Spot You Agree/Disagree with
	• Thinker's Chin (hand off chin when ready)		• Letter or Number Card Choices on a Metal Ring – A, B, C, D or 1, 2, 3, 4
	• Stand When You Are Ready		
	• Sit When You Are Ready	**Ranking**	• Rank with Your Fingers
	• Put your Pen on your Paper When Ready		• Rank with Your Arm (the higher, the better)
	• Put your Pen Down When You Are Finished		• Line Up According to Response
	• All Eyes on Teacher		• Knocking/Clapping/Cheering
	• Heads Down		

THE RESEARCH

USE TOTAL RESPONSE SIGNALS

Researchers agree that active learning produces the greatest success **(Echevarria & Graves, 2015)**. It is important to ensure that all learners, including those with limited L2 are able to participate in classroom instruction. The use of total response signals allows ELs to participate without having to be dependent on language. Likewise, it facilitates the informal assessment of students' academic and language skills development throughout the lesson. Using active response signals has a positive effect on student achievement when compared with passive responses **(Knapp & Desroachers, 2009)**. A research study by **Davis & O'neil (2004)** demonstrated that the use of response cards was highly effective with ELs, specifically with those who were also learning disabled.

Step 5: Use Targeted Visual and Vocabulary Strategies

Teachers everywhere fill their "bag of tricks" with as many strategies and tools as possible in order to help their students learn new material efficiently. Step Five is comprised of tools that make a huge impact on all students, especially struggling learners. Let's look at using visuals and vocabulary strategies and how they help us meet our teaching objectives effectively.

Use Visuals

Incorporating visuals in our lessons dramatically increases student ability to understand class lessons and discussions. It has been said that "a picture is worth a thousand words," and often this is true. Photos, maps, drawings, movie clips, and concrete objects give students access to content in spite of possible barriers such as lack of background on the subject or limited English proficiency. If the content objective, for example, is to explain safe lab procedures, showing photos of "safe" and "unsafe" activities will give students a stronger grasp of the content.

Another really effective visual tool is the graphic organizer. Graphic organizers provide a way for students to organize facts, ideas, and concepts that help them make sense of the content. You probably make use of some of these already. Graphic organizers can be used before instruction to provide a scaffold for new material, and they can show how much students already know about a topic. During instruction, they can be used to help students organize key information. After instruction, graphic organizers help students connect prior knowledge with new information and determine relationships between the two.

There are many types of graphic organizers that are available in books and on the Internet. Some of these include: story maps, Venn diagrams, spider maps, T-charts, and KWL charts. When introducing a new type of graphic organizer, be sure to model its use and provide time for guided practice. As students become more skilled at using the organizers, they can create their own variations.

One strategy that promotes the use of visuals and takes very little advance planning is Point and Talk. This strategy helps clarify meaning for new concepts. Simply draw or show a visual of the key concept for each lesson. Keep it posted throughout the unit

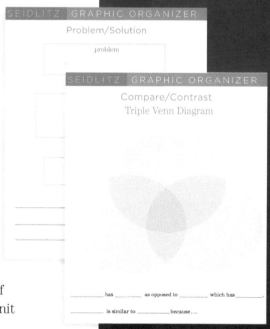

of study and consistently point back to it. Let's use a Language Arts concept to illustrate this strategy. When teaching plot development, use a mountain like the one below as a visual, and point to each stage as it is discussed. This gives students a visual anchor that will help simplify this vocabulary-dense concept.

Develop Vocabulary

In the introduction, we discussed the importance of incorporating academic vocabulary in all of our lessons. A good rule of thumb is to introduce and display at least two new words per lesson. Here are two specific strategies that build academic vocabulary:

SCANNING

Scanning is a powerful, quick, and efficient tool used to build academic language skills for students. This strategy teaches students essential words for understanding new content minutes before they encounter the words in a text. With this strategy, student achievement is increased by 33% as compared to students who did not use the strategy. Here's how it works:

1. The students survey a text from back to front looking for unfamiliar words.

2. The teacher generates a list of three to ten unfamiliar terms based on the students' survey.

3. The teacher writes short student-friendly definitions for the terms, giving definitions that match the way the word is used in the context of the passage.

4. The students practice pronouncing the words during a choral reading with the teacher.

5. The students read the passage.

6. The students use some of the words during the speaking and writing tasks in the lesson. For example, students might include scan words as they discuss the text with a partner, or they can use them in a written summary of the text.

Here's an example of how Scanning might sound in a typical classroom:

Teacher: *Provides students with handout containing word problems after modeling examples for the class.* Okay everyone, look at the handout, and let's do a quick scan of unfamiliar terms. Start at the bottom, scan toward the top, and circle two or more terms that you or someone else in class cannot define. *Students begin circling words on their handout.* Okay, I can see most of you have found a few words. Enrique, tell me one of the words you selected.

Enrique: Vehicle. *Teacher pauses and glances at poster saying, "Please express your thoughts in complete sentences."* I selected the word *vehicle*.

Teacher: *Writes down vehicle on dry erase board.* Thanks. Erica, what was one of the words you selected?

Erica: I selected the word *expression*.

Teacher: *Writes down the word expression on dry erase board.* Okay, does anyone else have a word that we should include? Brian?

Brian: I'm not sure what a *coordinate plane* is. I know we talked about it. Is that just like the graph we make of different problems?

Teacher: Kind of. Let's write that down too. *Writes coordinate plane.* Anyone else? Okay. Can anyone think of a short definition for the word *vehicle*? Just call out an answer.

Students: *A few students speak out loud.* A car, a truck. Something that moves you around.

Teacher: Let's write, "something that carries you around, like a car or truck." *Writes definition.* Okay, what does *expression* mean?

Students: *Calling out.* Equation, number sentence.

Teacher: Okay. Let's write, "a number sentence." That's what we usually have been calling expressions. *Writes definition.* Can someone raise a hand and tell me what a coordinate plane is?

Ted: Isn't a *coordinate plane* the plane that has all the x and y coordinates on it?

Teacher: Basically. Let's write something like, "the flat space with all the x and y coordinates."

Teacher: *At the end of the class period...* Okay, go ahead and fill out your math journals. Your sentence starter is on the board. Make sure you include at least one word from our scan: *vehicle, expression, or coordinate plane.*

When students read new written material, they often find unfamiliar vocabulary. To eliminate stumbling over new words, we use scanning before a reading exercise begins. It doesn't take very much time for students to get used to this procedure, and it quickly builds student understanding of academic vocabulary. Scanning gives students some control over the vocabulary we emphasize, and it gives us the chance to focus on learning what students don't know instead of re-emphasizing what they already do know.

MARZANO'S SIX-STEP PROCESS

In *Building Academic Vocabulary* (Marzano, 2004), Marzano outlines a comprehensive approach to learning the content-specific academic vocabulary, or the brick words that students encounter in their reading. The first three steps help us introduce new terms during the first lesson; the last three steps help students practice and reinforce those terms over time. These steps are easily remembered as the terms: *Describe, Describe, Draw, Do, Discuss, Play.*

Step 1 – Describe: Instead of giving a formal definition of a vocabulary word or term, teachers give students a description or explanation of the word or term using examples and visuals. The goal is to appeal to learners of all types in order to help them understand new vocabulary.

Step 2 - Describe: Ask students to give a description or explanation of a vocabulary word or term using their own words. By listening/reading student descriptions/explanations, we can assess mastery, or we can provide help to make the words comprehensible. Students record descriptions in their personal notebooks to reference later.

Step 3 - Draw: Ask students to draw a representation of the new vocabulary word or term. Acceptable ways to complete this task include: drawing pictures, designing symbols, making graphics, creating cartoons, finding a visual on the Internet or in a magazine. These tasks can be done individually or in groups.

Step 4 - Do: To give students more practice using new vocabulary words or terms, have them participate in activities such as: identifying prefixes, suffixes, synonyms, antonyms, related words, and additional visuals.

Step 5 - Discuss: Have students discuss the vocabulary words or terms as they work with/in partners, triads, or groups. This type of vocabulary discussion is more effective when it is structured. Additionally, monitoring student discussions clears up any confusion students may have about the words or terms.

Step 6 - Play: Students participate in games that reinforce deep understanding of the new vocabulary words or terms. Examples of games include: Jeopardy, Wordo (like bingo), Charades, Pictionary, Scrabble, etc.

Scanning and Marzano's Six-Step Process are two ways to teach vocabulary, but there are many other effective strategies. It doesn't matter which strategies we use as long as we remain focused on our goal: helping students develop a deep understanding of academic vocabulary so they can achieve in school and communicate in the real world.

While ELs benefit from all of Marzano's six steps, an enhanced approach focusing on what research has identified as specific needs is beneficial. ELs need teachers to focus on pronunciation, spelling, parts of speech, grammar, connotations, and contextual use (Dutro & Kinsella, 2010). The target for explicit instruction must have breadth and depth. Breadth of vocabulary knowledge refers to the understanding and familiarity of a multitude of words, including words used for related concepts. Depth of vocabulary knowledge refers to the understanding and familiarity of various common and uncommon meanings of a given word. Consider the multiple meanings for the word "order."

Order the following numbers from least to greatest.

The president gave the order to send U.S. troops to the Middle East.

Remember to place your t-shirt order by Friday.

Research also indicates that ELs do better when teachers focus explicitly on word parts (prefixes, suffixes, roots) and when they provide ELs with opportunities to make explicit links to cognates in their own language (Escamilla et al., 2010). The chart below lists ways teachers can implement Marzano's process in order to accommodate the unique linguistic needs of ELs.

MARZANO'S STEPS	FOR ELS	TEACHER/STUDENT
1. Provide a student-friendly description, explanation, or example of the new term.	• Pronounce the term, syllable by syllable • Have ELs write the term • Use native language to ensure understanding of the new term when possible • Explicitly reference or provide opportunity for students to make connections to relevant cognates • Identify word parts with cognate connections, if possible • Identify parts of speech and how the word is used • Provide visual examples and explanations	*This is the word ...* *It is pronounced...* *It is similar to the word ___. (native language term)* *Do you know any words in your language similar to ...?* *The parts of this word are...* *This prefix/root/suffix means ...* *Some examples are ...* *This word is a (noun, verb, adjective, etc.). Some examples of this word, in context, are ...*

2. Ask students to restate the description, explanation, or example in their own words.	• Model a conversation about a term with a partner
	• Allow students to discuss their terms with a partner using native and social language
	• Provide sentence stems for beginning ELs to write descriptions
	• Provide written models of word descriptions for students
	• Allow students to draw, label, and write descriptions in their native language and to use inter-language strategies, as needed
		Your conversation might sound like this:
		  The term ___ means...
		  It reminds me of ...
		  Your explanation of the term added is...

3. Ask students to construct a picture, symbol, or graphic representation of the term.	• Provide a model or representation of similar terms
	• Provide an opportunity for ELs to explain their drawing
	• Be aware that ELs may be making valid connections that need to be articulated because of a cultural difference
		Draw a picture representing...
		Explain to a neighbor why you represented ___ that way.
		You might use phrases such as:
		  I drew a....
		  To me it means ___because ...

MARZANO'S STEPS	FOR ELS	TEACHER/STUDENT
4. Periodically, engage students in structured vocabulary discussions that help them add to their knowledge of vocabulary items.	· Encourage students to connect terms to their own experiences inside and outside of school · Provide stems and model conversations during discussions	*Tell your partner why the term ___ is familiar to you. You can use the stem:* *____ reminds me of...* *I've seen the term ____ in/at ....*
5. Periodically, ask students to discuss the terms.	· Have ELs interact with L1 and L2 dominant peers during interactions where terms are discussed · Provide stems for comparing, contrasting, and constructing analogies	*See how the other members of your group explained the term ....* *Talk to your partner about the term ____ using the stems...* *____ is similar to/different from ____ because ....* *____ is to ____ as ____ is to ...*
6. Periodically, involve students in games that allow them to play with the terms.	· Make sure ELs of all proficiency levels are fully included in the games · Provide models and language stems, as necessary · Explain any hidden cultural expectations of games (volume, tone, competitive language, etc.)	*We're going to play ...* *During the game, you can use the phrases ...* *It should look like ....* *It should sound like ....*

Another strategy that supports teaching objectives is using sentence stems. This strategy helps students form complete sentences, and it allows students to grow accustomed to the kind of words and phrases usually found in academic English. Most importantly, however, sentence stems give students an opportunity to practice using new vocabulary words and terms in context. For example, when learning about the states of matter, this sentence stem, "One property of a solid is…" gives students the chance to practice using the words property and solid in the correct context. The process of using a sentence stem begins when the teacher provides it as a starting point for a response. Students can use sentence stems for oral and written responses.

At first, students will only use sentence stems when required to do so, but over time they quickly become a part of classroom routines.

There are two types of sentence stems, general and specific. A general stem can be used in any content area. We use general stems to find out what our students are thinking and also to determine the amount of background knowledge a student has on any given topic. Examples of general stems are: "I learned….," "I already know…," and "I agree/disagree with _____ because…" Unlike general stems, specific sentence stems are tied to a particular content area or lesson. We use specific stems to check for understanding of the learning objectives. Examples of specific stems are: "One cause of the Civil War was…," "Photosynthesis is…," "I think _____ is the protagonist because…" Using both general and specific sentence stems gives students many risk-free opportunities to speak and to write using academic language.

Examples include:

General Stem	Specific Stem
I learned …	I learned a new way to factor …
I already know …	I already know that authors use characterization to …
I agree/disagree with ___ because …	I agree/disagree with Dora the Explorer's decision to choose the iceberg because

We have also found it helpful to look at our assessments as a guide to developing sentence stems for students to use. Both standardized assessments and local assessments often have sentence structures and terminology that are unfamiliar to students. We can look at some of the assessment questions and then create sentence stems to give students a chance to practice using academic language.

Examples include:

Test Question	Sentence Stem
Which word from paragraph 2 means the same thing as sinister?	The word from the paragraph that means the same thing as sinister is …
What speed record did Alma exceed by exactly 4.66 miles per hour?	The record Alma exceeded by exactly 4.66 miles per hour was …
How did the invention of the printing press affect the flow of ideas in Europe in the 1500s?	The invention of the printing press affected the flow of ideas in Europe in the 1500's by …

Sentence stems provide a framework for students to gradually use increasing amounts of academic language. When our students have opportunities to practice using the words and phrases they will encounter on an assessment, they are better prepared for those assessments because the language used is familiar to them.

By strategically using general and specific sentence stems, we change the way students talk. When we change the way they talk, we open the door to new ways of thinking.

THE RESEARCH

USE TARGETED VISUAL AND VOCABULARY STRATEGIES

Graphic organizers are highly effecive when used appropriately. **Fountas and Pinnell (2001)** state that when content is illustrated with diagrams, the information will be better maintained over a period of time. **Meyen, Vergason, and Whelan (1996)** report that graphic organizers serve as an organized display that makes information easier to understand and to learn.

Students with learning disabilities often have difficulty recalling newly-learned content and with making connections between details and broad concepts. In addition, they often find that math facts and procedures can be very frustrating to learn and remember. **Maccini and Gagnon (2000)** found that using graphic organizers in math class may lessen students' difficulties with math concepts.

Pre-teaching terms enhances student reading comprehension. **Stahl and Fairbanks (1986),** demonstrate that student comprehension soars 33% when specific key terms are introduced prior to reading and learning (as cited in **Marzano, Pickering & Pollock, 2001**). Therefore, pre-teaching terms is important.

Using vocabulary strategies and sentence stems improve student achievement for ELs, who often find academic concepts especially difficult (**Echevarria, Vogt, & Short, 2017**).

Step 6: Have Students Participate in Structured Conversations

Step 6 focuses on creating opportunities for student conversation and discussion. Students who speak using the targeted language understand on a deeper level and create a "more durable memory trace" (Izumi, 2002).

Oral English fluency is not only conversational fluency; it is the ability to use academic language well enough to be academically competitive with English-speakers (Hakuta, Butler & Witt, 2000). The use of oral proficiency is important because it promotes access to the core educational curriculum and contributes to English literacy development (Goldenberg & Coleman, 2010). Current reports agree that a correlation exists between English oral proficiency and English literacy (reading and writing) skills (August & Shanahan, 2006). Consequently, educators must be more directive by structuring explicit language learning opportunities that develop academic English skills. These opportunities must provide ample practice using meaningful context (Goldenberg & Coleman, 2010). Teachers who facilitate a learning environment using structured conversations provide consistent and systematic oral language practice and support for ELs. Collaborative dialogue, in and of itself, is a source for learning a new language (Watanabe & Swain, 2007); it creates comprehensible output and enables students to internalize the language more efficiently.

Unstructured conversation is not considered an efficient means for helping ELs acquire academic language. According to Goldenberg & Coleman (2010), in order for ELs to be successful, they must have "productive verbal exchanges rather than simply finishing tasks." In heterogeneous classes, it is particularly important that ELs are adequately prepared to interact with their native English-speaking peers. Structuring conversation requires intentional decision-making on the part of the teacher. Teachers can structure conversations by specifying the content and function (purpose) of the discussion as well as the specific language form. Such interactions can take shape as whole class discussions, small group conversations, student-to-student exchanges, or discussions of varied length, ranging from brief responses to extended conversations. Different amounts of structure can be used in these exchanges, however all structures provide practice communicating in academic English with a pre-determined focus. The critical feature to remember when structuring conversations for ELs is to increase their English language proficiency. These interactions address what we know about ELs and their needs. ELs must ask and answer questions, summarize information, clarify ideas, offer/justify opinions, and compare/contrast viewpoints. Each of these language functions has certain phrases, language patterns, and grammatical structures associated with its form. Structured conversations

STRUCTURED CONVERSATIONS GIVE STUDENTS:

- practice acquiring new vocabulary.
- control of usage and conventions.
- comprehension of nuances in the language.
- interaction with others in different contexts, such as informal meetings, classroom discussions, and extended conversations.
- opportunities to tell or listen to stories.
- occasion to listen to or provide explanations of academic content.

provide students the opportunity to practice each of them. Teachers can frame conversations for students to practice as they ask and answer questions, state opinions (in sentences that begin with dependent clauses), or use complex sentences to compare two ideas. The fundamental goal of structured conversations is to allow students to "gain familiarity with new language forms, to hear other ways of describing academic concepts, and to hear themselves articulate an academic message" (Zweirs, 2008, p.132). Structured conversation can also be an effective vehicle for meeting the language objective of a lesson and for allowing students to interact and practice precise language skills stated in the objective. For example, if the language objective is: Students will ask and answer oral questions related to how the

U.S. responded to Soviet aggression using: "In response to _____, the U.S...." and "What was the effect of...?", then an effective way to facilitate and measure this language objective is for the teacher to model the structured conversation between students.

A simple strategy that weaves structured conversation into instruction is QSSSA (Question, Signal, Stem, Share, Assess). In this strategy, the teacher asks a question and the students give a response signal when they are ready to answer. Using a sentence stem, students are asked to share their responses with one or more peers. Lastly, the teacher assesses the quality of the discussion by selecting a few students to share their answers with the whole class. Students could also share by writing and then by reading their responses.

QSSSA Template

QUESTION
SIGNAL
STEM
SHARE
ASSESS

Simple Sample:

1. **(Question)** What effect did the explorations of Christopher Columbus have on contemporary society in Central America and the Caribbean?

2. **(Signal)** Please stand when you can finish this sentence.

3. **(Stem)** One effect of the explorations of Christopher Columbus on contemporary society in Central America and the Caribbean was...

    Wait for all students to show signal.

4. **(Share)** Beginning with a given sentence stem, students share their responses with a peer.

5. **(Assess)** The teacher randomly assesses students by calling on them individually.

Sample Signals:

Stand
Sit Down
Raise Your Right Hand
Raise Your Left Hand
Thinker's Chin

ementary Structured Conversation Example

QUESTION	SIGNAL ←→ STEM		SHARE	ASSESS
Math What is the sum of three and four?	Raise hand when ready to respond	The sum of three and four is …	Turn to Your Partner, Random Calling on Students	Students solve problems 1-5 in workbook
Social Studies Do you agree/disagree with Rosa Parks' decision to…?	Thinker's chin	I agree/ disagree with Rosa Parks' decision because…	Numbered Heads Together	Explain or illustrate, in journals, one thing you would have done
Science What is a characteristic of an insect?	Stand when ready	One characteristic of an insect is…	Think, Pair, Share	Label or illustrate some characteristics of insects
Language Arts What is the main idea?	Put your pen down when finished writing a response	The main idea is…	Inside Outside Circle	Randomize and rotate responses with whole group

econdary Structured Conversation Example

QUESTION	SIGNAL ←→ STEM		SHARE	ASSESS
Math What are some important things to remember when factoring equations?	Raise hand when ready to respond	One important thing to remember when factoring equations is… because…	Turn to Your Partner, Random Calling on Students	Students solve problems 1–5 in workbook
Social Studies Do you support/oppose Sam Houston's position on secession? Why?	Thinker's chin	I support/oppose Sam Houston's position because …	Numbered Heads Together	Students explain, in journals, one thing they would have done that is the same or different and why
Science What are some unusual characteristics of annelids?	Stand when ready	One unusual characteristic of annelids is… because…	Think, Pair, Share	Students label or illustrate characteristics of some insects
Language Arts What evidence shows that Stanley is/is not a hero?	Put your pen down when finished writing a response	Evidence that shows Stanley is/is not a hero includes …	Inside Outside Circle	Teacher randomizes and rotates responses with the whole group

General Sentence Stem Guide

Summarizing Learning	• I learned... • I now know...
	• I have discovered ...
	• I think the answer is...
	• Today, I realized...
	• Now I understand...
	• I can now teach someone to...
	• I still wonder...
	• I can now conclude...
	• The most significant thing I learned today was...
	• An important question I still have is...
	• I chose _____ because...
		• The significance of _____ is...
		• What I learned reminds me of...
		• I enjoyed learning about_____
		  because...
		• Today I learned that _____ is _____
		  because...
		• I would summarize my learning by saying...
		• My initial answer was _____ and now is
		  _____ because...
		• One thing I hope to learn next time is _____
		  because...

Sharing an Opinion	• I feel ... • I believe... • I wonder... • I think that... • I predict that... • I like the idea that... • The way I would... • In my experience... • My suggestion would be ... • What I understood is...	• One reason could be... • I like/dislike_____ because... • My initial reaction is _____ because... • My view on the matter is _____, because... • After thinking about _____, I...
Justifying an Opinion	• I think... • I like... • I would... • In my opinion... • I agree/disagree with... • My reasoning is ... • I conclude _____ because... • I support the_____ idea because... • _____supports the idea that....	• I think it might be _____ because... • I agree/disagree with _____ because... • Another idea might be _____ because... • I was thinking that _____ should be _____ because... • _____ corroborates the idea that...
Accessing Prior Knowledge	• I know... • I remember... • I recall... • In my experience... • This reminds me of... • I can connect this with... • One thing I want to remember... • One thing I have done before is... • One thing I know about_____ is...	• One question I have about _____ is ... • I'd like to know more about ... • One thing I'd like to know about ____ is ... • I would compare _____ to _____ because... • Discussing _____ made me think about...

Elaboration	• I would add... • I also believe...
	• I was thinking... • The way I would...
	• It is important because...
	• I chose _____ because...
	• You might also consider...
	• What I mean by _____ is...
	• The answer might also be ___ because...
		• I would agree/disagree with _____ be-
		  cause...
		• Another reason for_____ could be...
		• Another way of _____ is by...
		• I would elaborate on _____ by...
		• What I would add to _____ is _____ be-
		  cause...

New Vocabulary	• _____ means...
	• A new word from this _____ is...
	• I could use the word_____ when
	  discussing...
	• The word _____ reminds me of_____
	  because...
		• I remember seeing the word ____ when...
		• A synonym/antonym for the word ___ is...
		• Another word for _____ is...
		• The word _____ is an example of a...

T-Chart, Pair, Defend

This structured conversation allows students to approach a content concept from two opposing viewpoints.

1. Fill out a T-Chart with opposing points of view about a topic, as a class. For each point of view, write a sentence stem on the top of the column of the T-Chart.

2. Organize the students into pairs (A and B) and assign a point of view to each.

3. Have students use the stems and the notes taken on the T-Chart to defend their assigned point of view in a conversation. Students can either read the points directly off the chart or argue freely using their own words.

4. Ask a few students who used their own words to model their conversations in front of the class.

Here are some samples of possible topics and sentence starters.

Subject	Topic	Sentence Starters	
		A	B
Social Studies	Crusades	We should leave England for the Holy Land because ...	We should stay in England because ...
Science	The Use of Ethanol for Energy	We must convert America to an ethanol-based economy because ...	We should not convert America to an ethanol-based economy because ...
Language Arts	*The Three Little Pigs*	The wolf should blow all the houses down because...	The wolf should not blow all the houses down because...
Math	Setting up Word Problems	We should set up a table and make a sketch before setting up these equations because ...	We should not waste time setting up a table and making a sketch before setting up these equations because...
Art	Drawing With Perspective	It's easy to draw with perspective because...	It's difficult to draw with perspective because ...

Expert/Novice

This activity is especially suited for science and math classes because students often become confused about the processes involved in various steps/procedures in these subjects.

Here are the steps:

1. Students brainstorm questions a novice might ask about a procedure or process.

2. Students list possible answers an expert might give to the questions.

3. Students form pairs (A, B). One student plays the role of a novice, and the other student is the expert.

4. Ask a few students to model their conversations in front of the class.

The expert/novice activity becomes more engaging if students can take on different roles during the activity. They can be scientists at NASA talking to tourists or math tutors from a university talking to freshmen struggling with basic concepts. For some students, playing a formal role helps them feel less inhibited. At times, we have seen the model conversations that follow this activity involve humor and style. This makes the activity memorable to the students, and these conversations help build a sense of community in the classroom.

Written Conversation

In this strategy, students pass notes back and forth.

Here are the steps:

1. Identify two points of view. The two perspectives do not have to be opposed to each other. For example, we might have reasons a farmer would support a tariff and reasons a businessman might support a tariff.

2. Have students brainstorm a list of key vocabulary relevant to the topic.

3. Pair the students and assign one student for each perspective. Each pair has one piece of paper.

4. Give the students a sentence starter to begin the written conversation and have them write a sentence representing their point of view on a piece of paper. When finished, have students pass the note to their partners.

5. Have partners read what they wrote and then write a response. Students continue to pass the note back and forth writing about their topic for ten minutes.

6. Have student notes meet the following requirements:

   a. Each student writes one complete sentence each time the note is passed.

   b. Sentences must have capital letters and correct punctuation.

   c. Students are to use as many words as they can from the vocabulary brainstorm list or the word wall, and these words must be circled when the activity is concluded.

7. Select volunteers to read their written conversation to the class when the activity is finished. Structured conversations from multiple perspectives are easier to facilitate if students are accustomed to the first five steps. If they know what to say instead of "I don't know," speak in complete sentences, use response signals, and use sentence stems, they are better able to participate and stay focused during the interactions. The structured conversation format is a proven way to facilitate the use of academic language in the classroom. Also, conversations from multiple perspectives require students to use higher-level thinking skills that deepen the understanding of the concept they are studying. Structured conversations can be used as an integral part of everyday instruction.

THE RESEARCH

HAVE STUDENTS PARTICIPATE IN STRUCTURED CONVERSATIONS

Research supports the need to develop oral language proficiency for students who are learning English as a second language. "Oral English fluency" refers not just to conversational fluency, but also to fluency with academic language. That is, students should know English well enough to be academically competitive with native English-speaking peers (**Hakuta, Butler & Witt, 2000**). The use of oral proficiency is important because it promotes access to the core educational curriculum and contributes to English literacy development (**Goldenberg & Coleman, 2010**). Current research reports agree that a correlation exists between English oral proficiency and English literacy (reading and writing) skills (**August & Shanahan, 2006**). Educators must be more directive, structuring explicit language learning opportunities to develop academic English with ample opportunities for practice in meaningful context (**Goldenberg & Coleman, 2010**). Teachers, who facilitate a learning environment using structured conversations, provide ELs with consistent and systematic oral language practice and support.

Step 7: Have Students Participate in Structured Reading and Writing Activities

ELs need multiple opportunities in every content area to read and write in response to their learning. The more opportunities they have, the more proficient they become in the English language. According to research, effective reading instruction approaches – used with native speakers in the past –are also beneficial for ELs. The benefits, however, do not equal the same achievement for ELs as compared to native speakers (August & Shanahan, 2006). ELs require specific modifications and adaptations to increase literacy in reading and writing (August & Shanahan, 2010).

Making sure that ELs are familiar with the vocabulary and subject matter of content-area reading is more crucial than it is for native speakers. August and Shanahan (2010) focus on four significant distinctions for teachers to make when developing literacy in ELs:

• strategic use of reading

• enhanced instructional delivery routines

• adjustment for differences in knowledge

• more scaffolding

It is important for teachers to remember to accommodate reading and writing instruction for ELs linguistically, based on their level of language proficiency. For the early stage EL, it is helpful to provide native language and adapted text with a variety of visual and peer supports for reading. In writing, students at the beginning levels of proficiency do better when drawing or using their native language to express content concepts. Furthermore, student learning is enhanced when the teacher provides sentence stems with clear modeling.

Step 7 is about structuring these reading and writing activities so that students gain a deep understanding of content concepts. We create structure by clearly defining our purpose, our plan, and the process for each reading or writing activity.

Structured Reading Activities

All reading activities should be purpose-driven. In other words, we should be able to answer this question: Why am I having my students read this? We derive purpose from content objectives and the state standards for each subject. Therefore, aligning the reading activity with the content objective gives us a clear purpose for the assignment. Once the purpose for the reading activity is defined, we need to make a plan. Asking, "How will I make sure my students are ready to read this?" helps the planning process. We need to decide whether students are ready to read the text independently; if they are not, supports need to be put in place to ensure success. To prepare students to read independently, we can establish prior knowledge of the reading assignment, scan the text for unfamiliar words, and allow students to partner-read the text. When students read an assignment, it is good to customize the selection of a structured reading activity because the goal is to ensure student success. Specifically, we want to think about what strategies students will use to make sense of the text. Different types of texts require diverse strategies. The thinking that goes on while reading a fairy tale is very different from the thinking required when reading a word problem in math class. Here is a specific strategy that help students understand various texts:

...EBODY-WANTED-BUT-SO STRATEGY

Somebody-Wanted-But-So strategy (Macon, Bewell, & Vogt, 1991) is
...d during or after reading to help students understand literary elements
...h as conflicts and resolutions. It is also a great summarization technique
...ocial studies, since so much of world history is based on the wants and
...ds of humans. Students determine the main character (somebody), his/her
...ivation (wanted), the main conflict (but), and the resolution to the conflict

...mebody	Wanted	But	So
Big Bad Wolf	Pigs for dinner	They hid in the brick house.	He went hungry.
...e Frank	To hide from the Nazis	Someone turned her in.	She died in a concentration camp.

...r examples of Structured Reading Activities include:

...ading Activity	Description
...P2RS ("...queepers")	This is a classroom reading strategy that trains students to use cognitive and metacognitive strategies to process nonfiction text. The steps are: Survey, Question, Predict, Read, Respond, and Summarize (Echevarria, Vogt, & Short, 2017).
...nell Notes	This is a method of note-taking in which paper is divided into two columns. In one large column, students take traditional notes in outline form. In the second column, students write key vocabulary terms and questions (Pauk, 2013).
...a Bookmarks	In this activity, students take reflective notes on bookmark-sized pieces of paper. The bookmarks include quotes, observations, and words from the reading that strike the reader as interesting or effective (Samway, 2006).
...ert Method	In this activity, students read texts with a partner and mark the texts with the following coding system: a "✓" to show that a concept or fact is already known, a "**?**" to show that a concept is confusing, a "**!**" to show something is new or surprising, or a "**+**" to show an idea or concept that is new (Echevarria, Vogt, & Short, 2017).

Structured Reading Activities

PURPOSE Why am I (the teacher) having the EL read this text, and how does it support the objectives?	
PLAN How will I make connections between what the EL knows and what will be read? What will the student need to know to read and to understand the passage completely? What resources does an EL need to access before reading?	
PROCESSES What resources will the EL use while reading? What process and/or learning strategy will the EL use while reading? How will the EL demonstrate comprehension of what was read? How will the EL reflect on material that was read? How will the EL reflect on the effectiveness of individual reading skills?	

Structured Writing Activities

Much like reading activities, the first step in creating structured writing activities is to determine why students need to write. Specifically, we want to define how the writing task will help students gain understanding of the content objective. For example, if a science objective requires students to explain the differences between the three states of matter, the writing assignment needs to support that goal.

The second step for creating a structured writing activity is to ask, "Can my students successfully complete the writing task on their own?" If the answer is no, then supports that lead to writing independence need to be put in place. Modeling is a very effective strategy, and all students benefit from explicit modeling of the writing task. In a think-aloud strategy, we verbalize the thinking that goes on in the writer's mind while writing. This helps establish a common ground for writers and demystifies the writing process for students. Alternative strategies include establishing prior knowledge and using sentence frames. This technique reminds students about more ideas to use in writing. Providing sentence and paragraph frames gives students more language to use to begin writing. The more ideas and language students have before they begin to write, the more independent and confident they become as writers.

Lastly, we decide on a specific writing strategy, structure, or process that reinforces the content goals. Writing activities range from informal written responses on sticky notes to formal research reports with presentations.

Here are two examples of structured writing activities:

RAFT (ROLE, AUDIENCE, FORMAT, TOPIC)

This writing strategy enables students to write from various points of view, using different genres, topics, and audiences. The strategy works well in all subjects, especially in language arts. RAFT (Fisher & Frey, 2007) is also highly engaging for students in content-area classrooms because it injects creativity into sometimes dull concepts. RAFT stands for Role (the perspective the student takes), Audience (the individuals the author is addressing), Format (type of writing that will take place, and Topic (the subject of the writing). We can select all four categories for students, or allow students to self-select some or all of them.

Some examples include:

Class	Role	Audience	Format	Topic
Language Arts	myself	classmates	narrative	summer vacation
Math	triangle	other shapes	persuasive speech	why I can't be a square
Science	Sir Isaac Newton	students	letter	laws of motion
Social Studies	Native American chief	younger tribesman	how to	survive (find food, shelter, clothing, protection)
Physical Education	fifth grader	first-grade class	list	expectations in gym

EXPERT WRITING

This strategy involves students taking on the role of "expert" for a given topic, concept, or unit of study. An effective way to introduce this strategy is to have all students find an area in which they are already an expert (cleaning their room, irritating their siblings, making macaroni and cheese, etc.) and to complete the expert writing process with that topic before moving to academic concepts. When ready to tackle an academic topic, students brainstorm (individually or with partners) the questions that someone would ask an expert relating to their area of expertise. For example, an expert on the Civil War might be asked the following things: Who fought in the Civil War? Why were the states fighting? Who won the Civil War? During the unit of study, or individual lesson, the student makes notes about the answers to those questions. The student then writes an explanation or description of the topic or concept including all of his or her "expert knowledge." Expert writing works across all content areas and grade levels. Including an Expert/Novice Conversation (see Appendix) during the brainstorming phase helps generate more ideas.

Processes for Understanding and Accessing Information from Texts

READING		
Scaffolding for Reading	Cooperative Reading	Independent Reading
Adapted Text	Anticipation Chat	Book Reviews
Advance Organizers	Genre Analysis/Imitation	Comprehension Strategies
Anticipation Guides	Insert Method	Cornell Notes
Building Background	Instructional Conversation	Double Entry Journals
Graphic Organizers	Literature Circles	Field Notes
Margin Notes	Numbered Heads Together	Guided Notes
Native Language Text	Partner Reading	Idea Bookmarks
SQP2RS	Prediction Café	Outlining
Think-Alouds	QtA (Question the Author)	SSR Program
Taped Text	Reader, Writer, Speaker, Response Triads	Summarization Frame
Related Literature (including native language texts)	Reciprocal Teaching	
Scanning	SQP2RS	
	Structured Conversation	

Processes for Preparing and Providing Opportunities for Writing

WRITING		
Scaffolding for Writing	Cooperative Writing	Independent Writing
Building Background	Dialogue Journals	First-Person Narratives
Concept Definition Map	Graffiti Write	Expository Writing: Summarization Description Sequence Cause and Effect Comparison
Concept Mapping	Native Language Brainstorm	
Draw and Write	Peer Editing	
Free Write	Reader, Writer, Speaker, Response Triads	Double Entry Journals
Graphic Organizers	Read, Write, Pair, Share	Draw and Write
KWL	Sentence Mark Up (with a partner)	Field Notes
Native Language Brainstorm	W.I.T. Questioning	Free Write
Paragraph Frames	Written Conversation	Guided Notes
Sentence Frames		Journals
Sentence Sort		Letters/Editorials
Summarization Frames		Perspective-Based Writing
Think-Alouds		R.A.F.T.
Quick Write		Tickets Out
		Writing in Native Language (depending on program model)

THE RESEARCH

HAVE STUDENTS PARTICIPATE IN STRUCTURED READING AND WRITING ACTIVITIES

Research has shown that the approaches we have used historically for effective reading instruction with native speakers are also beneficial for ELs. Research also tells us, however, that those benefits still do not lead to the same achievement for ELs compared to native speakers. ELs require modifications and adaptations to increase the opportunity for increased literacy in the area of reading **(August & Shanahan, 2006)**. For young learners, it is necessary to teach the components of reading explicitly, such as phonics, phonemic awareness, vocabulary, and fluency, just as we do for native speakers. On the other hand, for students in the middle elementary grades and higher, the emphasis shifts to vocabulary and fluency to support comprehension **(August & Shanahan, 2006)**. What is also critical for these students is the relationship between content familiarity (background knowledge) and text comprehension. Teachers of ELs must make explicit connection to what learners know and what they are expected to read. English speakers use reading as an opportunity to learn, while English Learners must be familiar with the content they are reading if the material is to be comprehensible **(Goldenberg & Coleman, 2010)**.

APPENDIX

Seven Steps for a Language-Rich, Interactive Classroom
Walk-Through Form

Teacher: _____

Period/Subject: _____

Date: _____

Content Objective: _____

Language Objective: _____

☐ Teacher/Student Interaction
☐ Student/Student Interaction
☐ Independent Task

STEP	MEASURABLE EVIDENCE

1 **Teach students strategies and language to use when they don't know what to do.**
• Instruction 2.4 – Differentiation
• Learning Environment 3.2 – Managing Student Behavior
	☐y ☐n Language learning strategies observed (instructed, clarified, or emphasized)
	   ☐ reading _____ (examples, etc.)
	   ☐ writing _____ (examples, etc.)
	   ☐ listening _____ (examples)
	   ☐ speaking _____ (IDK, scaffolded stems)
	☐y ☐n Students respond or use helping strategy and then respond
	☐y ☐n Students accomplish learning task or use helping strategy and then accomplish learning task

2 **Have students speak in complete sentences.**
• Instruction 2.3 – Communication
	☐y ☐n Expectation of complete sentences is clearly displayed
	   ☐ Students use complete sentences - # of students _____
	   ☐ Teacher prompts students to use complete sentences

3 **Randomize and rotate when calling on students.** • Planning 1.3 – Knowledge of Students • Learning Environment 3.1 – Classroom Environment, Routines & Procedure • Learning Environment 3.3 – Classroom Culture	☐y ☐n System is established for randomizing/rotating ☐ Variety of students respond- # of students_____
4 **Use total response signals.** • Planning 1.2 – Data & Assessment • Instruction 2.3 – Monitor & Adjust	☐y ☐n Teacher has students use total response signals tied to content and language objectives for the lesson ☐ All students respond with response signal

5 **Use visuals and vocabulary strategies that support your objectives.**
• Planning 1.1 – Standards & Alignment
• Instruction 2.2 – Content Knowledge & Expertise
	☐y ☐n Awareness of language proficiency of ELs is evident
	   ☐ Documentation of language levels
	☐y ☐n Content and language objectives are clearly displayed
	   ☐ Objectives align to standards (content and ELP)
	   ☐ Objectives include academic/language task
	   ☐ Objectives are shared orally at the beginning and at the end of the lesson
	☐y ☐n Terms (related to objective) posted with linguistic/nonlinguistic explanation
	   ☐ Terms are explicitly explained, clarified, or emphasized
	☐y ☐n Stems (aligned to objective) are clearly displayed
	   ☐ Stems are aligned/differentiated to students' language proficiency levels
	☐y ☐n Stems are introduced/modeled/practiced

6 **Have students participate in structured conversation.**
• Planning 1.4 – Activities
• Learning Environment 3.3 – Classroom Culture
	☐y ☐n Structured opportunities allow students to engage in conversation aligned to objectives
	Teacher/student interaction is aligned to objectives observed
	   ☐ Questions asked are aligned to objectives
	   ☐ Balance of opportunity exists for student responses
	Student/student interaction observed
	   ☐ Conversation is aligned to objectives
	   ☐ Structures ensure that all students speak
	   ☐ Students use posted vocabulary/stem in appropriate context

7 **Have students participate in structured reading and writing activities.**
• Planning 1.2 – Data & Assessment
• Planning 1.4 – Activities
• Instruction 2.2 – Achieving Expectations
	☐y ☐n Assigned reading task is aligned to the objective
	   Type of task _____
	☐y ☐n Assigned writing task is aligned to the objective
	   Type of task _____

Stems and Activities Aligned to the ELPS

	STEMS	ACTIVITIES
1(A) use prior knowledge and experiences to understand meanings in English	**Prior Knowledge** • I know .... • I want to know ... • This word/phrase might mean ... • This word/phrase is like ... • This word/phrase reminds me of ... • I think this word probably means ... because...	• Anticipation Chat • Anticipation Guides • Free Write • Insert Method • KWL • List/Sort/Label • Pretest with A Partner
1(B) monitor oral and written language production and employ self-corrective techniques or other resources	**Self-Corrective Techniques** • I mean ... • Let me say that again ... • I meant to say/write ... • Let me rephrase that ... • How would I be able to check ...?	• Accountable Conversation Stems • Oral Scaffolding • Think-Alouds • Total Response Signals
1(C) use strategic learning techniques such as concept mapping, drawing, memorizing, comparing, contrasting, and reviewing to acquire basic and grade-level vocabulary	**Memorizing/Reviewing** • ___ means... • I know/don't know the words ... • I'm familiar/not familiar with ___ • I will need to review ... **Concept Map/Drawing** • The main idea/key term of my concept map/ drawing is ... • Some examples/important details are ... • I decided to represent ____ this way because ... **Comparing/Contrasting** • ___ is the same as ___ because they are both ... • ___ is different from __ because ... • ___ is similar to ___ because ... • ___ is different from ___ because... • One significant similarity is ___ because ...	• Concept Map • Creating Analogies • Flash Card Review • Four Corners Vocabulary • Personal Dictionary • Scanning • Six-Step Vocabulary Process • Total Response Signals • TPR • Vocabulary Game Shows • VSS • Word Play

	STEMS	ACTIVITIES
1(D) speak using learning strategies such as requesting assistance, employing non-verbal cues, and using synonyms and circumlocution (conveying ideas by defining or describing when exact English words are not known)	**Requesting Assistance** • Can you help me ... • I don't understand ... • Would you please repeat/rephrase that...? • Would you please say that again a little slower? • Would you please explain ...? **Synonyms/Circumlocution** • It's the same as ... • It has ... • It's similar to ... • It includes ... • Let me rephrase that ...	• Accountable Conversation Stems • Expert/Novice • Instructional Scaffolding • Think, Pair, Share • Total Physical Response
1(E) internalize new, basic and academic language by using and reusing it in meaningful ways in speaking and writing activities that build concept and language attainment	**Concept Attainment with New Words** • I think ___ is a ... • I think ___ is not a ... • All ___ are ... • All ___ have ... • All ___ are not ... • All ___ do not have ... • ___ is an example of ___ because... • ___ is not an example of ___ because ... • Another example might be ___ because .... • One characteristic/attribute of ___ is ... **Language Attainment with New Words** • ___ means ... • ___ does not mean ... • I can use the word ___ when ... • I would not use the word ___ when ... • I might be able to use the word ___ when ___ because ... • I probably would not use the word ___ when ___ because ...	• Concept Attainment • Concept Definition Map • Creating Analogies • Group Response with a White Board • Instructional Conversation • Question, Signal, Stem, Share, Assess • Socratic Discussion • Think, Pair, Share • Whip Around
1(F) use accessible language and learn new and essential language in the process	**Using Accessible Language** • If I want ___ I need to say ... • To find out how to say __ I can look ... • Will you please explain what ___ means? • I can use resources such as ___ to remember how to say ...	• Accountable Conversation Questions • CALLA Approach • Expert/Novice • Instructional Scaffolding • Think Alouds

	STEMS	ACTIVITIES
1(G) demonstrate an increasing ability to distinguish between formal and informal English and an increasing knowledge of when to use each one commensurate with grade-level learning expectations	**Formal and Informal English** • At school we say … • When we talk to the whole class we should … • When we talk with our friends we can … • Scientists/Historians/Mathematicians/Writers use the word/phrase … to say… • I would describe someone outside of school by … • I would describe that concept using scientific/social studies/mathematical/literary language by saying …	• Brick and Mortar Cards • Discussion Starter Cards • Formal/Informal Pairs • Radio Talk Show • Same Scene Twice • Sentence Sort
1(H) develop and expand repertoire of learning strategies such as reasoning inductively or deductively, looking for patterns in language, and analyzing sayings and expressions commensurate with grade-level learning expectations	**Deductive Reasoning** • All ___ are … • ___ is ___ so it must be an example of … **Inductive Reasoning** • All the ___ we saw were/had … • So all ___ probably are/have • Every example we observed was/had … • So we can infer that all ___ are/have … **Patterns in Language** Analyzing Sayings/Expressions • I think the word/expression ___ means… • One word/expression that was used a lot was… • The writer chose this word/expression because… • Another expression the writer could have chosen might be… because … • I noticed the writer tended to use (tense, mood, structure, etc.) … • One pattern I noticed was …	• Instructional Conversation • Literature Circles • Perspective-Based Learning • Question, Signal, Stem, Share, Assess • Structured Conversation

	STEMS	ACTIVITIES
2(A) distinguish sounds and intonation patterns of English with increasing ease	**Sounds and Intonation Patterns** • You said the word ___. It starts with... • I think that word starts with the letter/is spelled ___ because ... • You stressed the word ___ because ... • You did not stress the word ___ because ... • To change the meaning of this sentence, I could stress ... • To change the tone of this sentence, I could...	• CCAP • Segmental Practice: tongue twister; syllable, storm, say; native language comparisons • Sound Scripting • Supra-segmental Practice: list stressed words, recasting, pronunciation portfolio, content/function word comparisons
2(B) recognize elements of the English sound system in newly acquired vocabulary such as long and short vowels, silent letters, and consonant clusters	**Sound System** • The word ___ has the long/short vowel ... • The word ___ has a silent ... • The word ___ has the consonant blend ... • The letter ___ in the word ___is long because ... • The ___ is silent in the word ___ because... • The word ___ is pronounced ___ because ...	• Songs/Poems/Rhymes • Sound-Based Word Sorts • Word Wall Based on Sounds
2(C) learn new language structures, expressions, and basic and academic vocabulary heard during classroom instruction and interactions	**Language Structures/Expressions during Interactions** • I heard the new word/phrase... • One new phrase I used was ... • I heard ___ use the word/phrase ... • A new word/phrase I heard was ... • I can use that word/phrase when ... • I used the word/phrase ___ when I spoke with ... • I used the word/phrase ___ to express the idea that	• Oral Scaffolding • Personal Dictionary • Scanning • Self-Assessment of Vocabulary Understanding • Think, Pair, Share • Vocabulary Self-Collection • Word Sorts
2(D) monitor understanding of spoken language during classroom instruction and interactions and seek clarification as needed	**Clarification during Instruction and Interaction** • Can you help me to ...? • I don't understand what/how... • Would you please repeat that? • So you're saying ... • May I please have some more information?	• Inside/Outside Circle • Instructional Conversation • Instructional Scaffolding • Structured Conversation • Think-Alouds • Think, Pair, Share • TPR

	STEMS	ACTIVITIES
2(E) use visual, contextual, and linguistic support to enhance and confirm understanding of increasingly complex and elaborated spoken language	**Linguistic, Visual, Textual Support** • If I want to find out ___, I can ... • I can use ___ to check if I .... • When I hear ___, it tells me ... • If I don't understand ___ I can say things like ... • Will you please explain what ___ means? • Let me see if I understand. You said ... • Would you please show me... on the (diagram/picture/organizer/notes/etc.)?	• Graphic Organizers • Inside/Outside Circle • Instructional Conversation • Instructional Scaffolding • Nonlinguistic Representations • Posted Phrases and Stems • Structured Conversation • Think, Pair, Share
2(F) listen to and derive meaning from a variety of media such as audio tape, video, DVD, and CD ROM to build and reinforce concept and language attainment	**Concept Attainment from a Variety of Media** • I notice ... • I heard/saw a ... • I heard/observed ___ which makes me think ... • I think ___ is an example of ___ because... • One characteristic/attribute of ___ that I heard/observed is ... **Language Attainment from a Variety of Media** • I heard/saw the word/phrase ___. • I think the word/phrase means/does not mean ... • I heard/saw the word/phrase ___ . I can use it when... • I heard/saw the word/phrase ___. I might be able to use it when___ because ... • I heard/saw the word/phrase___. I probably would not use it when ___ because ...	• Chunking Input • Concept Attainment • Concept Mapping • Journals • Learning Logs • Pairs View • Visual Literacy Frames

	STEMS	ACTIVITIES
2(G) understand the general meaning, main points, and important details of spoken language ranging from situations in which topics, language, and contexts are familiar to unfamiliar	**Meaning in Spoken Language** • I think ___ means … • You said___. I think it means … • I think ___means ___ because … • I heard you say___. Another way to say that might be… **Main Point in Spoken Language** • It's about… • I think the main idea I heard was … • Based on the information I heard in ___, I can conclude that the main points were … • (The speaker) said _____which supports my view that the main idea is … **Details in Spoken Language** • I heard the speaker say … • One thing the speaker said was … • One important thing I heard the speaker say was … • The speaker said ____which is important because … • I heard the speaker say ___which supports the idea that…. • One thing I heard was …	• Dramatic Play • IEPT • Instructional Conversation • Literature Circles • Perspective-Based Activities • Question, Signal, Stem, Share, Assess • Reciprocal Teaching • Socratic Dialogue • Story Telling • Structured Conversation • Summarization Frames
2(H) understand implicit ideas and information in increasingly complex spoken language commensurate with grade-level learning expectations	**Implicit Ideas** • I think ___ probably … • I can infer ___ probably … • I can assume ____ because … • Even though it doesn't say ___, I think … • Based on ___, I can infer that … • From the information found in ___, I can infer that ___ because …	• Instructional Conversation • Literature Circles • Perspective-Based Activities • Question, Signal, Stem, Share, Assess • Reciprocal Teaching • Socratic Dialogue • Story Telling • Structured Conversation • Summarization Frames • Whip Around

	STEMS	ACTIVITIES
2(I) demonstrate listening comprehension of increasingly complex spoken English by following directions, retelling or summarizing spoken messages, responding to questions and requests, collaborating with peers, and taking notes commensurate with content and grade-level needs	**Following Spoken Directions** • The first step is … • The next steps are … • I know I'm finished when … • The initial step is … • The next step(s) in the process is/are … • I know I've completed the task successfully when … **Retelling/Summarizing Spoken English** • It's about… • The main idea is … • First…. Then…. Finally… • I would explain the story/concept to a friend by … • The general idea is… • Some ideas I heard that support the main idea include… **Responding to Questions/Requests** • I heard you say____, so I need to …. • You asked____. • I think … • I think you're asking … • One answer to your question might be … **Collaborating With Peers** • Can you help me understand …? • Would you please repeat that? • Who's responsible for…? • Who should …? • My job/part/role is to… • So I should … • I'm responsible for … **Taking Notes** • I noted … • The main ideas I wrote down were … • Some details I wrote down were … • I can organize the ideas I wrote by…(making an outline, concept map, Venn diagram, chart, etc.)	• Framed Oral Recap • IEPT • Instructional Conversation • Keep, Delete, Substitute, Select • Literature Circles • Note Taking Strategies • Outlines • Perspective-Based Activities • Question Answer Relationship (QAR) • Question, Signal, Stem, Share, Assess • Reader/Writer/Speaker Response Triads • Reciprocal Teaching • ReQuest • Story Telling • Structured Conversation • Summarization Frames • Tiered Questions • Tiered Response Stems • W.I.T. • Word MES Questioning

	STEMS	ACTIVITIES

3(A) practice producing sounds of newly acquired vocabulary such as long and short vowels, silent letters, and consonant clusters to pronounce English words in a manner that is increasingly comprehensible	**Producing Sounds**
	
	• The letter(s) ___ make(s) the ___ sound.
	• The word ___ begins with the letter...
	• The word ___ has the long/short vowel ...
	• The word ___ has a silent ...
	• The word ___ has the consonant blend ...
	• The letter ___ in the word ___is long because ...
	• The ___ is silent in the word ___ because...
	• The word ___ is pronounced ___ because ...
		• Content/Function Word Comparisons
		• Fluency Workshop
		• List Stressed Words
		• Pronunciation Portfolio
		• Recasting
		• Segmental Practice:
		  -Tongue Twisters
		  -Syllable Storm
		  -Native Language
		  -Comparisons
		• Supra-segmental Practice

3(B) expand and internalize initial English vocabulary by learning and using high-frequency English words necessary for identifying and describing people, places, and objects, by retelling simple stories and basic information represented or supported by pictures, and by learning and using routine language needed for classroom communication	**Description and Simple Story Telling with High-Frequency Words and Visuals** • I see ... • I hear ... • I observe ... • ___ has/is ... • The picture(s) show(s) ... • The first thing that happened was...Then... Finally... • ___ probably also has/is... • ___ could be described as___ because ... **Routine Language for Classroom Communication** • Where is/are...? • Where do I...? • How do I ...? • Can you help me ....? • May I please have some more information? • May I ask someone for help? • May I go to...? • May I sharpen my pencil? • When is it time to ...?	• Accountable Conversation Stems • Conga Line • Content-Specific Stems • Expert/Novice • Inside/Outside Circle • Instructional Conversation • Literature Circles • Numbered Heads Together • Partner Reading • Question, Signal, Stem, Share, Assess • Retelling • Somebody, Wanted, But, So, Then • Summarization Frames • Think, Pair, Share

STEMS	ACTIVITIES
3(C) speak using a variety of grammatical structures, sentence lengths, sentence types, and connecting words with increasing accuracy and ease as more English is acquired	**Speak Using A Variety of Structures**	• Canned Questions

3(C) speak using a variety of grammatical structures, sentence lengths, sentence types, and connecting words with increasing accuracy and ease as more English is acquired

Speak Using A Variety of Structures

DESCRIPTION
- _____ is/has/looks like ...
- _____ is/has/looks like __ because ....
- _____ tends to/seems/becomes/is able to/ appears to be...
- _____ is an example of.... because ...
- _____ shows/is/has ___ which means...
- _____ for example/for instance/such as....

SEQUENCE
- _____ while/before/after ...
- First,...second...finally...
- At first...but now/later/subsequently....
- Previously/initially/earlier...however now/later...

CAUSE AND EFFECT
- _____ causes ...
- When ___then...
- Not only___ but also...
- _____ was brought about by...
- _____ was one of the causes of ___ however...
- _____ contributed to ___ due to ...

COMPARISON
- _____ is the same as/is different from ...
- _____ differs from/is similar to ___ in that...
- Although ___ still/yet...
- _____ however/whereas/nevertheless...
- _____ on the other hand/on the contrary ...

QUALIFICATION
- Sometimes/few/many ...
- Occasionally/often/seldom/rarely...
- Sometimes/often___ because...
- Many/few___ however/due to......
- Rarely/seldom ___ yet ...

EMPHASIS
- _____ is important.
- _____ is significant due to ...
- It's important to note... since...
- _____ is especially relevant due to ...
- Above all/of course/remember ___ because...

CONCLUSION
- Finally/therefore...
- As a result___ should/it is necessary to ...
- _____ proves ___ because...

ACTIVITIES
- Canned Questions
- Instructional Conversation
- Experiments/Labs
- Discovery Learning
- Literature Circles
- Numbered Heads Together
- Peer Reading/Tutoring
- Perspective-Based Activities
- Question, Signal, Stem, Share, Assess
- Reader/Writer/Response Triads
- Signal Words
- Simulations
- Socratic Dialogue
- Story Telling
- Structured Conversation
- Summarization Frames
- You Are The Teacher

	STEMS	ACTIVITIES
3(D) speak using grade-level content area vocabulary in context to internalize new English words and build academic language proficiency	**Speak Using Grade-Level Vocabulary** • This word/phrase means … • This word/phrase is like … • This word/phrase reminds me of … • I think this word probably means … because…	• Content Specific Stems • Creating (and Sharing) Analogies • Instructional Conversation • Literature Circles • Perspective-Based Activities • Question, Signal, Stem, Share, Assess • Reciprocal Teaching • Self-Assessment of Levels of Word Knowledge • Structured Conversation
3(F) ask and give information ranging from using a very limited bank of high-frequency, high-need, concrete vocabulary, including key words and expressions needed for basic communication in academic and social contexts, to using abstract and content-based vocabulary during extended speaking assignments	**Ask and Give Information** • What is…? • ___ is … • What did you notice about/in…? • I noticed … • How do you … • First you … then… • Why do you think ____ is important? • ___ is important because… • What are the characteristics/attributes of …? • One of the characteristics/attributes of ___ is … • What do you think caused …? • I think ___ caused ___ because… • In my opinion ___ happened due to…	• Instructional Conversation • Interview Grids • Literature Circles • Peer Reading/Tutoring • Perspective-Based Activities • Question, Signal, Stem, Share, Assess • Socratic Dialogue • Structured Conversation • Think, Pair, Share
3(G) express opinions, ideas, and feelings ranging from communicating single words and short phrases to participating in extended discussions on a variety of social and grade-appropriate academic topics	**Express Opinions, Ideas, and Feelings** • How do you feel when/about…? • I feel… • What do you think about …? • I think… • What is your opinion about…? • In my opinion… • My view on the matter is… • I agree/disagree that___ because… • Why do you think…? • I think___ because… • Is there another… • Another ___ might be___ since … • What else can you tell me about ..?	• Anticipation Chat • Instructional Conversation • Literature Circles • Perspective-Based Activities • Question, Signal, Stem, Share, Assess • Reciprocal Teaching • Socratic Dialogue • Structured Conversation • Think, Pair, Share • W.I.T. Questioning
3(H) narrate, describe, and explain with increasing specificity and detail as more English is acquired	**Narrate, Describe, and Explain with Increasing Detail** • This is a … • ___ is about… • The main idea is … • It's important to remember… • First…. then…. finally… • Initially….then… ultimately… • It's significant that …because… • Some of the supporting ideas are… • Some of the important details include…	• Instructional Conversation • Literature Circles • Numbered Heads Together • Peer Reading/Tutoring • Perspective-Based Activities • Question, Signal, Stem, Share, Assess • Socratic Dialogue • Someone, Wanted, But, So, Then • Story Telling • Structured Conversation • Summarization Frames

	STEMS	ACTIVITIES
3(I) adapt spoken language appropriately for formal and informal purposes	**Formal and Informal Spoken English** • At school we say … • When we talk to the whole class we should … • When we talk with our friends we can … • I would explain the story/concept to a friend by … • Scientists/Historians/Mathematicians/Writers use the word/phrase … to … • I would describe ___ to someone outside of school by … • I would describe ___ using scientific/social studies/mathematical/literary language by …	• Expert/Novice • Oral Language Scaffolding • Radio Show • Sentence Sort • Word Sort
3(J) respond orally to information presented in a wide variety of print, electronic, audio, and visual media to build and reinforce concept and language attainment	**Concept Attainment from a Variety of Media** • I see… • I noticed … • I heard/saw a … • I heard/observed, which makes me think … • I think ___ is an example of ___ because… • One characteristic/attribute of ____ that I heard/observed is … **Language Attainment from a Variety of Media** • I see/hear… • I heard/saw the word/phrase ___. • I think the word/ phrase means/does not mean … • I heard/saw the word/phrase ___ . I can use it when… • I heard/saw the word/phrase ___. I might be able to use it when___ because … • I heard/saw the word/phrase___ I probably would not use it when ___ because …	• Chunking Input • Concept Attainment • Concept Definition Map • Journals • Learning Logs • Pairs View • Visual Literacy Frames

	STEMS	ACTIVITIES
4(A) learn relationships between sounds and letters of the English language and decode (sound out) words using a combination of skills such as recognizing sound-letter relationships and identifying cognates, affixes, roots, and base words	**Decoding** • The letter(s)___ make(s) the ___ sound... • The word ___ has the long/short vowel ... • The word ___ has a silent ... • The word ___ has the consonant blend ... • The letter ___ in the word ___is long because ... • The ___ is silent in the word ___ because... • The word ___ is pronounced ___ because ... **Cognates** • A cognate is ... • The word ___ sounds like ___ in my language and means ... • The word ___ sounds like___ in my language, but does NOT mean ... **Affixes, Roots, and Base words** • A prefix is... • A suffix is ... • An affix is ... • A root is... • A base word is... • The word___ has the prefix___ which means... • The word ___ has the suffix ___ which means... • The word ___ has the root___ which means ... • The root ____ is probably common in history/geography/science/math/language arts because ... • This word probably means ___ because...	• Direct Teaching of Affixes • Direct Teaching of Cognates • Direct Teaching of Roots • Self-Assessment of Levels of Word Knowledge • Word Generation • Word Sorts • Word Study Books • Word Walls
4(B) recognize directionality of English reading such as left to right and top to bottom	**Directionality of English Text** • In English, words go ... (students can use gestures to indicate directionality) • In ____ (Chinese/Arabic/Hebrew, etc.) words go..., but in English, words go... • In __(Spanish/French/Russian, etc.) words go...., and in English, words also go...	• Directionality Sort • Total Physical Response (TPR)

	STEMS	ACTIVITIES
4(C) develop basic sight vocabulary, derive meaning of environmental print, and comprehend English vocabulary and language structures used routinely in written classroom materials	**Sight Vocabulary/ Environmental Print** • When I see the word/phrase ___ it means... (students demonstrate actions with gesture or use simple phrases to explain classroom vocabulary) • This sign says ___; it tells me......(students demonstrate actions with gesture or use simple phrases to explain classroom vocabulary) • My friend's name is ... • Our logo/mascot/team is ...	• Expert-Novice Role Play • Oral Scaffolding • Total Physical Response
4(D) use prereading supports such as graphic organizers, illustrations, and pre-taught topic-related vocabulary and other prereading activities to enhance comprehension of written text	**Prereading Supports** • This story/article is about ... • This word list tells me this story is about ... • The illustrations tell me this story is about ... • The diagram tells me the story is about ... • The organizer tells me that I should pay attention to ... • The organizer shows me that ___ is significant because ... • The strategy that will help me to understand this text the best is probably.... (note taking; scanning; surveying key text features, such as bold words, illustrations, and headings; using the word list, etc.)	• Advance Organizers • Anticipation Guides • Backwards Book Walk • Comprehension Strategies • DRTA • Scanning • SQ2PRS • Visuals • Word Walls
4(E) read linguistically accommodated content area material with a decreasing need for linguistic accommodations as more English is learned	**Use of Linguistically Accommodated Material** • ___ (native language summary, native language word list, picture dictionary, outline, simplified English text, sentence starters, etc.) helped me to understand/write/say ... • I should use ___ when ... • I don't need to use ___ when...	• Adapted Text • Comprehension Strategies • Hi-Lo Readers • Insert Method • Margin Notes • Native Language Texts • Outlines and Graphic Organizers • Related Literature • SQ2PRS • Stop and Think • Taped Text

	STEMS	ACTIVITIES
4(F) use visual and contextual support and support from peers and teachers to read grade-appropriate content area text, enhance and confirm understanding, develop vocabulary, grasp language structures, and tap background knowledge needed to comprehend increasingly challenging language	**Using Visual/Contextual Support to Understand Text** READING • The illustrations tell me this text is about … • The diagram tells me the text is about … • The organizer tells me that I should pay attention to … • The organizer shows me that ___ is significant because … CONFIRMING UNDERSTANDING • I can check if I understand what I'm r eading by… • The strategy that will help me understand this text the best is probably…. (note taking; scanning; surveying key text features, such as bold words, illustrations, and headings; using the word list, etc.) because… DEVELOPING VOCABULARY AND BACKGROUND KNOWLEDGE • I use the word wall/word list while I read to … • When I come across an unfamiliar word or phrase, I … GRASP OF LANGUAGE STRUCTURES • When I see ___ in a text, it tells me…. • I noticed a lot of ____ in the text. It probably means… • I also noticed___ in the text. I was wondering… because … • I noticed the writer tended to use (tense, mood, structure, etc.) … **Using Teacher/Peer Support to Understand Text** READING • What is the main idea of …? • What should I write down about …? • What should I pay attention to in …? • Would you please show me on the (diagram/picture/organizer/notes/etc.)….? CONFIRMING UNDERSTANDING • It seems like ___. Is that right? • Can you help me understand…? • Can I please have more information about …? • Where can I find out how to …? • Can I ask someone for help with…?	• Anticipation Chat • Comprehension Strategies • DRTA • Graphic Organizers • Improv Read Aloud • Insert Method • Nonlinguistic Representation • Perspective-Based Activities • QtA • Question, Signal, Stem, Share, Assess • Scanning • SQ2PRS

	STEMS	ACTIVITIES
4(F) *continued*	DEVELOPING VOCABULARY AND BACKGROUND • Will you please explain what ___ means? • Does ___ also mean ...? • Why does the text have ....? GRASP OF LANGUAGE STRUCTURES • One word/expression that I saw was... • What does the word/expression ____ mean? • Why is there a lot of ____ in the text?	
4(G) demonstrate comprehension of increasingly complex English by participating in shared reading, retelling or summarizing material, responding to questions, and taking notes commensurate with content area and grade-level needs	**Shared Reading** • Can you help me understand ...? • Would you please repeat that? • Who should read ...? • I will read ... • My job/part/role is to... • So I should ... • I'm responsible for ... **Retelling, Summarizing** • It's about... • The main idea is ... • First.... Then.... Finally... • I would explain the story/concept to a friend by ... • The story is about___ • What happened was... • The general idea is... • Some ideas I heard that support the main idea include... **Responding to Questions/Requests** • I heard you say___, so I need to .... • You asked___. • I think ... • I think you're asking ... • One answer to your question might be ... **Taking Notes/ Responding to Questions** • I noted ... • The main ideas I wrote down were ... • Some details I wrote down were ... • I can organize the ideas I wrote by...(making an outline, concept map, Venn diagram, chart, etc.)	• Cornell Notes • Dramatic Play • Guided Notes • Instructional Conversation • Keep, Delete, Substitute • Literature Circles • Numbered Heads Together • Perspective-Based Activities • Question, Signal, Stem, Share, Assess • Reciprocal Teaching • Socratic Dialogue • Story Telling • Structured Conversation • Summarization Frames

	STEMS	ACTIVITIES
4(H) read silently with increasing ease and comprehension for longer periods	**Read Silently with Increasing Comprehension** • I read about ... • I liked/didn't like ... • The text I read today described ... • I would describe what I read today as... because...	• Book reviews • Dialogue Journal • Double Entry Journal • Idea Bookmarks • Interactive Reading Logs • SSR Program • Structured Conversation
4(I) demonstrate English comprehension and expand reading skills by employing basic reading skills such as demonstrating understanding of supporting ideas and details in text and graphic sources, summarizing text, and distinguishing main ideas from details commensurate with content area needs	**Supporting Ideas** • The text talked about things like ... • The text discussed different topics, for example ... • ____ supports the idea that... • ____ resulted in .... • ____ caused/led to ____ **Details** • This talks about things/people/events like ... • ____ could be described as... • I would describe ____ as___ because.... • Some significant features/facts about ____ include... **Graphic Sources** • The illustrations tell me this text is about ... • This illustration/chart/diagram shows ... • The illustrator showed ____ by... • The author(s) included a diagram/graph/chart showing ____ because ... • This illustration/diagram/graph/chart is significant because ... **Summarizing** • This is about ... • The main characters/ideas are ... • The main actions/arguments/problems discussed in the passage are ... • In my opinion, the most significant idea/conflict in this passage is ____ because... **Distinguishing Main Ideas and Details** • This text is about ... • The main idea of this text is ... • One detail that supports the main idea is ... • ____ supports the idea that .... • ____ is an example of a detail because... • ____ is an example of a main idea because ...	• Comprehension Strategies • DRTA • Graphic Organizers • Learning Logs • Nonlinguistic Representation • Numbered Heads Together • Perspective-Based Activities • QtA • Question, Signal, Stem, Share, Assess • Scanning • SQ2PRS • Structured Conversation Following Reading • Summarization Frames

	STEMS	ACTIVITIES
4(J) demonstrate English comprehension and expand reading skills by employing inferential skills such as predicting, making connections between ideas, drawing inferences and conclusions from text and graphic sources, and finding supporting textual evidence commensurate with content area needs	**Predicting** • I think ___ will.... • I predict ___ will happen next because... • Based on the information in the passage, it seems that ___ will probably.... • ____ supports the idea that ___ might... **Making Connections Between Ideas** • ___ reminds me of ... • ___ is similar to ... • ___ is different from ... • ___ relates to what happened when ___ because... • ___ is the result of __ because... **Drawing Inferences and Conclusions** • I think ___ probably ... • I can infer ___ probably ... • I can assume ____ because ... • Even though it doesn't say ___, I think ... • Based on ___, I can conclude that ... • From the information found in ___, I can infer that ___ because ... **Finding Supporting Textual Evidence** • I think___ because ... • ____ supports the idea that ... • I think ___ is evidence that ... • ___ corroborates the idea that ... • Based on the information found in ____ I can conclude that __ because...	• Comprehension Strategies • DRTA • Graphic Organizers • Learning Logs • Nonlinguistic Representation • Perspective-Based Activities • Prediction Café • Question, Signal, Stem, Share, Assess • QtA • Scanning • Summarization Frames • SQ2PRS • Structured Academic Controversy • Structured Conversation

	STEMS	ACTIVITIES
4(K) demonstrate English comprehension and expand reading skills by employing analytical skills such as evaluating written information and performing critical analyses commensurate with content area and grade-level needs	**Evaluating Written Information** • The theme of this text is... • The setting/plot/conflict/genre of this text is... • Some characters/ideas/symbols/metaphors/similes found in this text include ... • I would describe ___ as ___ because.... • The author used ___ in order to... • The author could have used ___ in order to ... **Performing Critical Analysis** • The author wrote this to ... • The author used the word/phrase ___ to... • The intended audience of this text is ... • The writer's motive for ___ was probably ... • The writer tried to prove ___ by... • ___ is an example of bias/propaganda because ... • The author was successful/unsuccessful because ... • I would agree/disagree with the author that ___ because...	• Book Reviews • Comprehension Strategies • Dialogue Journals • Double Entry Journals • DRTA • Graphic Organizers • Instructional Conversation • Learning Logs • Logs and Journals • Nonlinguistic Representation • Perspective-Based Activities • QtA • Question, Signal, Stem, Share, Assess • Scanning • SQ2PRS • Structured Academic Controversy • Structured Conversation following Reading • Summarization Frames

	STEMS	ACTIVITIES
5(A) learn relationships between sounds and letters of the English language to represent sounds when writing in English	**Letter/Sound Relationships in Writing** • The letter(s)___ make(s) the ___ sound. • The word ___ has the long/short vowel ... • The word ___ has a silent ... • The word ___ has the consonant blend ... • The letter ___ in the word ___is long because ... • The ___ is silent in the word ___ because... • The word ___ is pronounced ___ because ...	• Homophone/Homograph Sort • Word Generation • Word Sorts • Word Study Books • Word Walls
5(B) write using newly acquired basic vocabulary and content-based grade-level vocabulary	**Write using New Vocabulary** • I learned the word... • ___ means.... • I can use the word ___ to ... • I can use the phrase ___ in order to show ... • The phrase ___ can be used to help the reader... • The word/phrase ___ would/would not be appropriate for ... • I can ___ using the word/phrase...	• Choose the Words • Cloze Sentences • Dialogue Journals • Double Entry Journals • Field Notes • Letters • Learning Logs and Journals • Read, Write, Pair, Share • Self-Assessment of Levels of Word Knowledge • Think, Pair, Share • Ticket Out • Word Sort • Word Wall
5(C) spell familiar English words with increasing accuracy, and employ English spelling patterns and rules with increasing accuracy as more English is acquired	**English Spelling** Patterns and Rules • ___ is spelled ... • ___ begins with the letter ... • In this set of words I notice ... • These words are all similar because ... • The spelling rule that applies to this word is ___ because ... • This word is spelled correctly/incorrectly because ... • I can check my spelling by ...	• Homophone/Homograph Sort • Peer Editing • Personal Spelling Guide • Word Analysis • Word Sorts • Word Walls
5(D) edit writing for standard grammar and usage, including subject-verb agreement, pronoun agreement, and appropriate verb tenses commensurate with grade-level expectations as more English is acquired	**Grammar and Usage** • Pronouns agree when ... • The subject ___ agrees/disagrees with the verb___ because... • The pronoun ___ agrees/disagrees with ___ because... • The present/past/future/conditional tense is appropriate/inappropriate in this sentence because ...	• Contextualized Grammar Instruction • Daily Oral Language • Oral Scaffolding • Peer Editing • Reciprocal Teaching • Sentence Mark Up • Sentence Sorts • Writing Process

	STEMS	ACTIVITIES
5(E) employ increasingly complex grammatical structures in content area writing commensurate with grade-level expectations, such as: (i) using correct verbs, tenses, and pronouns/ antecedents; (ii) using possessive case (apostrophes) correctly; and (iii) using negatives and contractions correctly	**Using Correct Verb Tenses** • A subject of a sentence is... • A verb is... • A subject and a verb agree when... • A verb tense is... • A tense is appropriate when... **Using Possessive Case/Contractions Correctly** • An apostrophe is... • Apostrophes are used to show... • A contraction is... • The apostrophe in this contraction is correct/ incorrect because... • This apostrophe correctly/incorrectly shows a contraction because... **Using Negatives** • The word (no/not/none) is used when... • An example of a sentence with (no/not/none) is... • Neither is used when... • An example of a sentence with neither is... • Hardly, scarcely, and barely are used to show... • Nothing, nowhere, and nobody are used to show...	• Contextualized Grammar Instruction • Daily Oral Language • Oral Scaffolding • Peer Editing • Reciprocal Teaching • Sentence Mark Up • Sentence Sorts • Writing Process

	STEMS	ACTIVITIES
5(F) write using a variety of grade-appropriate sentence lengths, patterns, and connecting words to combine phrases, clauses, and sentences in increasingly accurate ways as more English is acquired	**Writing Using a Variety of Sentence Structures** CAUSE AND EFFECT • ___ caused/led to ... • When ___ then... • Not only___ but also... • ___ was brought about by... • ___ was one of the causes of ___, however... • ___ contributed to ___ due to... COMPARISON • ___ is the same as/is different from ___ • ___ differs from/is similar to ___ in that... • Although ___ still/yet... • ___however/whereas/nevertheless... • ___on the other hand/on the contrary ... QUALIFICATION • Sometimes/few/many... • Occasionally/often/seldom/rarely... • Sometimes/often___ because... • Many/few___ however/due to...... • Rarely/seldom ___ yet ... EMPHASIS • ___ is important. • ___ is significant due to ... • It's important to note... since... • ___ is especially relevant due to... • Above all/of course/remember ___ because... CONCLUSION • Finally/therefore... • As a result___ should/it is necessary to ... • ___ proves ___ because...	• Dialogue Journals • Double Entry Journals • Draw & Write • Field Notes • Free Writes • Genre Analysis & Imitation • Hand Motions for Connecting Words • Letters/Editorials • Logs and Journals • Modified Writers Workshop • Perspective-Based Writing • RAFT • Read, Write, Pair, Share • Sentence Frames • Summary Frames • Writing Process
5(G) narrate, describe, and explain with increasing specificity and detail to fulfill content area writing needs as more English is acquired	**Narration** • First,...second...finally... • ___ while/before/after ... • At first...but now/later/subsequently.... • Previously/initially/earlier...however now/late... **Description & Explanation** • ___ is/has ___ • ___is tends to/seems/becomes/is able to/appears to be... • ___ is an example of....because ... • ___ shows/is/has ___, which means... • ___ for example/for instance/such as.... • ___ is a characteristic or attribute of ___	• Book Reviews • Dialogue Journals • Double Entry Journals • Draw & Write • Field Notes • Free Writes • Genre Analysis/Imitation • Letters • Logs and Journals • Perspective-Based Writing • Sentence Frames • Target/Native Language Write • Unit Study • Unit Study for ELs • Writing Process • Writing Scaffolds

Guide to Terms and Activities

The terms and activities listed below provide an additional resource for teachers who want to increase student engagement and achievement in their classrooms. Included in the list is a brief description of the activity and citations to reference additional information. Becoming familiar with the terms and implementing the activities with students will transform any classroom into a language-rich interactive classroom.

Academic language: AAcademic language is specialized vocabulary. Its structures tend to be more abstract, complex, and challenging and are found with high frequency in classroom oral and written discourse.

Accountable Conversation Questions:

Place the following poster in your room: Model the way students can use the poster questions when they are unsure about what to say when called on by the teacher (Seidlitz & Per-ryman, 2011). Students should know that they do not have to say, "I don't know." Instead, they can ask for more information, more time to think, a repetition of the question, a place to find more information, or the assistance of a friend. Newcomer English Learners should not be pressured to speak in front of the class if they have not yet begun to show early production levels of speech/language proficiency. Students should be encouraged, but not forced, to speak when in the silent period of language development (Krashen, 1982).

> **What to say instead of "I Don't Know"**
>
> • May I please have some more information?
>
> • May I have some time to think?
>
> • Would you please repeat the question?
>
> • Where could I find information about that?
>
> • May I ask a friend for help?

Adapted Text: Adaptations in text helps struggling students comprehend academic language. Some methods include: graphic organizers, outlines, highlighted text, taped text, margin notes, native language texts, native language glossaries, and word lists (Echevarria, Vogt, & Short, 2017).

Advance Organizers: Information given prior to reading or instruction helps students organize information they encounter during instruction (Mayer, 2003). Advance organizers should activate prior knowledge and help organize new infor-

mation. Examples include: graphic organizers, anticipation guides, KWL, guided notes, etc.

Affective Filter: This is the emotional barrier to language acquisition caused by a negative perception or response to one's environment.

Anticipation Chat: Prior to instruction, a teacher facilitates a conversation between students about the content to be learned. The teacher opens the discussion by having students make inferences about what they are going to learn based on prior knowledge, experiences, and limited information about the new concepts (Zwiers, 2008).

Anticipation Guides: This is a structured series of statements given to students before instruction. Students choose to agree or disagree with the statements either individually or in groups. After instruction, students revisit the statements to discuss whether they have changed their minds about the statements. New learning can often inform and change student opinion (Head & Readence, 1986).

Backwards Book Walk: Students scan a nonfiction text, briefly looking at headings, illustrations, captions, key words, and other text features before reading a book. After the scan, students discuss what they believe they will learn from the text (Echevarria, Vogt, & Short, 2017).

Book Reviews: Students read and examine book reviews. After being immersed in the book review genre, English Learners write short reviews, which can be published for others to read (Samway, 2006).

Brick Words: Brick words are content specific vocabulary (Dutro & Moran, 2003).

Brick and Mortar Cards: Students are given five "brick" cards with academic vocabulary (content-area terms) and are instructed to organize them in a way they think makes sense. Afterward, they have to link the cards together using "mortar" words. Mortar words tie the language together.

Students may need lists of sentence terms and connecting words to facilitate the process (Zwiers, 2008).

CALLA Approach (Cognitive Academic Language Learning Approach): This approach to teaching English Learners requires explicit instruction in language learning strategies, academic content, and language skills through scaffolding, active engaged learning, and language use (Charmot & O'Malley, 1994).

CCAP (Communicative Cognitive Approach to Pronunciation): This five step process helps English Learners improve pronunciation skills (Celce-Murcia, Brinton, & Goodwin, 1996, as cited in Florez, 1998). The steps include the following:

• Description and analysis of the pronunciation feature

• Listening/discrimination activities (See Segmental/Supra-Segmental Practice in this guide)

• Controlled practice and feedback

• Guided practice and feedback

• Communicative practice

Canned Questions: Students are given a series of question stems ranging from the lowest to the highest level of Bloom's Taxonomy in order to participate in discussions about a topic. For example:

• "What is...?"

• "How do...?"

• "What would be a better approach to...?"

• "How do you know that...?" (Echevarria, Vogt, & Short, 2017)

Card Sort: In this activity, students are given a set of cards with pictures and/or words and asked to sort them into categories. Sample categories resemble the following: living vs. nonliving, states of matter, types of energy, etc. While students are sorting the cards, they ask their group members questions like:

• What does this picture show?

• What category would be good for this card?

• How can we be sure these cards all go together?

• Which rule are we using to categorize this card?

Carousel Activity: In this activity, groups are assigned to stations in the classroom. Each station has a set of questions, and students are given a specified time to answer the questions. Groups rotate from station to station until they have answered all questions. This activity encourages interaction among students.

Chat Room: In this writing activity, students use informal and formal English to describe terms and concepts. Each student is given a paper outline of a computer screen and a term or concept. On the computer screen, students describe the term or concept by writing a text message using informal English. Students then switch computer screens with a partner. The partners rewrite the text message using formal English.

Choose the Words: During this activity, students select words from a word wall or word list to use in a conversation or in writing.

Chunking Input: Chunking means to break-up material into smaller units for easier comprehension. Visual and auditory information can be chunked so that students have time to discuss new information, pay attention to details, and create schema for organizing new information.

Cloze Sentences: Fill-in-the-blank sentences help students process academic text (Taylor, 1953; Gibbons, 2002).

Compare, Contrast, Analogy, Metaphor, and Simile Frames: These sentence frames help students organize schema for new words (Marzano et al., 2001; Hill & Flynn, 2006).

For example:

• Compare: ___ is similar to ___ in that both....

• Contrast: ___ is different from ___ in that ...

• Analogy: ___ is to ___ as ___ is to ____

• Metaphor: I think _____ is.....

• Simile: I think ___ is like/as... because...

Comprehension Strategies: Comprehension strategies help proficient readers understand what they read. These strategies can be used for different kinds of text, and when they are taught, students are more likely to use them. Strategies include: prediction, self-questioning, monitoring, note-taking, determining importance, and summarizing (Echevarria, Vogt, & Short, 2017; Dole, Duffy, Roehler, & Pearson, 1991; Baker, 2004).

Concept Attainment: This Jerome Bruner strategy instructs teachers to provide examples and non-examples of concepts to students. Then teachers can ask students to categorize the examples. Over time, students learn to categorize at increasing levels of depth and understanding (Boulware & Crow, 2008; Bruner, Goodnow, & Austin, 1956).

Concept Definition Map: This visual organizer enables students to process a term (Echevarria, Vogt, & Short, 2017). Four questions are asked:
• What is the term?
• What is it?
• What is it like?
• What are some examples?

Concept Mapping: This is a technique for making a visual diagram of the relationship between concepts. Concept maps begin with a single concept written in a square or circle in the center of a page. New concepts are listed and connected with lines and shapes creating a web that shows the relationship between the ideas (Novak, 1995).

Conga Line: During this activity, students form two lines facing one another. Students in each line share ideas, review concepts, or ask one another questions. After the first discussion, one line moves and the other remains stationary so that each student can converse with a new partner (Echevarria, Vogt, & Short, 2017).

Content-Specific Stems: In this activity, sentence stems using content specific vocabulary are provided to students. For example, instead of a general stem such as, "In my opinion...," a content specific stem would be, "In my opinion the Declaration of Independence is significant because..."

Contextualized Grammar Instruction: Teaching grammar in mini-lessons demonstrates specific, meaningful tasks that students can transfer to writing or speaking. The purpose of the grammar instruction is to enable students to communicate verbally and to write more effectively (Weaver, 1996).

Cornell Notes: Students use this method of note-taking in which a paper is divided into two uneven columns. In one large column, students take traditional notes in modified outline form. In the smaller column, students write key vocabulary terms and questions (Pauk, 2013).

Creating Analogies: This method is used to generate comparisons using the frame: ____ is to ____ as ___ is to ____ (Marzano, Pickering, & Pollock, 2001).

Creating Words: This vocabulary game provides an opportunity for students to review key vocabulary by using words in creative ways. To start, a student selects a word and rolls a cube that has the following on its sides: model it, draw it, act it out, write it, talk about it, etc. Based on the outcome of the rolled cube, the student represents the word, and the classmates guess the word.

Daily Oral Language: During a five-minute mini-lesson, students view a list of sentences with incorrect English usage. Students learn correct usage by correcting the mistakes in the sentences (Vail & Papenfuss, 1993).

Dialogue Journal: A dialogue journal is exchanged between the student and teacher or between two or more students. The journal focuses on academic topics, and the language used by the teacher and student should be content focused and academic (Samway, 2006).

Direct Teaching of Affixes: During this activity, students build knowledge of English word structures by learning prefixes and suffixes (White, Sowell, & Yanagihara, 1989).

Direct Teaching of Cognates: These lessons include words that sound the same in the primary language and the target language. For a list of Spanish and English cognates, see: www.colorincolorado.org/pdfs/articles/cognates.pdf

Students must be careful of false cognates, words that sound the same in the primary and target language, but do not have the same meaning. For a list of false Spanish/English cognates, see: www.123teachme.com/learn_spanish/false_cognates

Direct Teaching of Roots: These lessons teach the Greek and Latin roots that form the base of many English words. A partial list of roots can be found here: www.msu.edu/~defores1/gre/roots/gre_rts_afx2.htm

Directed Reading-Thinking Activity (DRTA): During reading, the teacher stops regularly to have students make and justify predictions. Questions might be: What do you think is going to happen? Why do you think that will happen next? Is there another possibility? What made you think that? (Echevarria, Vogt, & Short, 2017).

Directionality Sort: In this activity, students sort texts in various languages on perceived directionality. Is the text written from top to bottom, then left to right? Is the text right to left, then top to bottom? For more ideas to teach this concept, see: ot.eku.edu/sites/ot.eku.edu/files/files/Directionality.pdf

Dirty Laundry: This vocabulary activity helps students extend their knowledge of newly acquired words/terms. Students are given one vocabulary word or content concept and an outline of a paper t-shirt. On one side of the t-shirt, students write a message about their assigned word, without using the word. On the reverse side of the t-shirt, students draw a picture of the word/term. The aim of this activity is to have other students in class guess the word described on the t-shirt. T-shirts can be displayed on classroom walls or hung using clothespins (Created by Cristina Ferrari, Brownsville ISD).

Discovery Learning: This is an inquiry-based approach to instruction in which teachers create problems and dilemmas through which students construct knowledge. Ideas, hypotheses, and explanations continue to be revised while learning takes place (Bruner & Kalnins, 1973). This discovery approach has been criticized by some (Marzano et al., 2001; Kirschner, Sweller, & Clark, 2006) for teaching skills to novices who don't have adequate background and language to be able to learn new content. Teachers of English Learners must be careful to pre-teach content-area functional language and set goals and objectives for the lesson when using the discovery approach.

Discussion Starter Cards: Small cards containing sentence starters are given to students to use when beginning an academic conversation or when seeking ways to extend a conversation. For example: "In my opinion...," "I think...," "Another possibility is...," etc. (Thornbury, 2005).

Double Entry Journals: This is a two-column journal used for reflective writing about texts. In one column, students write words, phrases, or ideas they found interesting or significant while reading. In the other column, students write the reasons they found the words significant, or they list ways they could use them in their own writing (Samway, 2006).

Draw & Write: This exercise allows English Learners to express their knowledge of academic content while drawing and writing. Students may use their native language to express ideas but are encouraged to express new concepts using English (Adapted from Samway, 2006).

Experiments/Labs: This is a form of discovery learning in science where students directly encounter the scientific process: making an observation, forming a hypothesis, testing the hypothesis, and coming to a conclusion. Teachers of English Learners need to make sure to pre-teach necessary content and functional vocabulary to enable full participation of ELs.

Expert/Novice: This is a simulation involving two students. One student takes on the role of an expert and the other a novice in a particular situation. The expert responds to questions asked by the novice. The procedure can be used for lower level cognitive activities, such as having students

introduce one another to classroom procedures or for higher-level activities, such as explaining content-area concepts in depth. The procedure can also be used to model the difference between formal and informal English, with the expert speaking formally and the novice informally (Seidlitz & Perrryman, 2011).

Field Notes: Field notes are notes/reflections written in journals when studying new content. Field notes can be written or drawn and should be content focused. They can contain both social and academic language (Samway, 2006).

First-Person Narrative: When writers write from their own point of view, they are writing from the first-person. When writing in the first-person, writers use the pronoun, "I."

Flash Card Review: To engage in this exercise, students make flash cards that include definitions and illustrations of words. Students can study, play games, and sort the flash cards in various ways.

Fluency Workshop: In triads, students take turns listening and speaking to one another about the same topic. Each student has one turn to speak, while the others listen. When listening, students may ask questions, but they cannot contribute an opinion about the speaker's words. After the activity, students evaluate their level of fluency to see how levels improved from the beginning to the end of the workshop (Maurice, 1983).

Fold the Line: For this activity, students line up chronologically based on a predetermined characteristic such as height, age, number of pets, etc. Then the line folds in half upon itself, providing each student a partner. Students are then asked to formulate a response/answer to a task or question. Depending on the task/question, students use formal or informal English to share responses with partners (Kagan, 1992).

Formal/Informal Pairs: The teacher writes a statement on two strips of paper; one with formal English, one with informal English. The teacher distributes one strip to each student. Students have to find their match in the classroom.

Four Corners Vocabulary: This is a way of processing vocabulary using a paper or note card divided into four sections: term, definition, sentence, and illustration (Developed by D. Short, Center for Applied Linguistics. Described in Echevarria, Vogt, & Short, 2017).

Framed Oral Recap: This is an oral review involving two students using sentence starters. Students are given stems such as: "Today I realized...," "Now I know....," and "The most significant thing I learned was ...." Students pair up with a partner to discuss what they have learned in a lesson or unit (Adapted from Zwiers, 2008).

Free Write: During free write, students write nonstop about a topic for five to ten minutes. The goal is to keep writing, even if they can't think of new ideas. They may write, "I don't know what to write," if they are unable to think of new ideas during the free write. English Learners can sketch and write in their native language although they should be encouraged to write in English (Elbow, 1998).

General Stems: These are incomplete sentences that scaffold the development of language structures to provide the opportunity for conversation and writing in any academic context.

Genre Analysis/Imitation: Students read high quality selections from a genre of literature during this activity. They note particular words, phrases, and ideas they found interesting or effective and record those in a journal. Students then use their notes and observations as a resource when writing in that genre (Adapted from Samway, 2006).

Glossary Circles: This activity is based on the idea of Literature Circles (Daniels, 1994). In this activity, students work collaboratively on a set of related terms. They are given one glossary page per term, using a template that includes four squares labeled Vocabulary Enrichment, Illustration, Connections, and Discussion Questions. During learning, students share terms, illustrations, definitions, connections, and questions that have been added to the glossary page.

Graffiti Write: In small groups, students are asked to simultaneously list academic words tied to a particular concept, within a short time frame.

Graphic Organizers: Graphic organizers are a form of nonlinguistic representation that can help students process and retain new information. They provide a way of developing a learner's schema by organizing information visually. Examples include the T-Chart, Venn diagram, Concept Map, Concept Web, Timeline, etc. (Marzano, Pickering, & Pollock, 2001).

Group Response with a White Board: During this activity, students write responses to questions on white boards using dry erase markers. These can be made from card stock slipped into report covers, or with shower board cut into squares that fit on student's desks. White boards are a form of active response signal shown to be highly effective in improving achievement for struggling students.

Guess Your Corner: This activity provides a way to review/assess student comprehension of key content concepts. To begin, post four previously introduced terms/content concepts around the classroom. Give each student a characteristic, attribute picture, synonym, etc. for one of the four terms/content concepts. Students are responsible for guessing the correct concept.

Guided Notes: Teacher prepared notes used as a scaffold help students practice note-taking skills during lectures. For examples of guided note formats see: www.studygs.net/guidednotes.htm

Hand Motions for Connecting Words: Gestures representing transition/signal words help students visually model the function of connecting words in a sentence. For example, students might bring their hands together for terms like: also, including, as well as, etc. For terms such as excluding, neither, without, no longer, etc., students could bring their hands together. Students can invent their own signals for various categories including: comparing, contrasting, cause and effect, sequence, description, and emphasis (Adapted from Zwiers, 2008).

Hi-Lo Readers: While reading books are published on a variety of reading levels, they can have the same content focus and objective. For samples, see the National Geographic Explorer Books found on these websites: http://new.ngsp.com/Products/SocialStudies/nbspnbspNationalGeographic-ExplorerBooks/tabid/586/Default.aspx and http://www.kidbiz3000.com/

History Scene Investigation (HIS): The teacher presents a covered image of an historical scene. The image is slowly uncovered while students make and record observations and predictions. This activity can be used as a discussion starter for a pre-writing activity (Seidlitz & Perryman, 2011).

Homophone/Homograph Sort: The teacher prepares homophone/homograph cards, listing words that sound the same, but are spelled differently, e.g., know/no, hear/here. The teacher asks the students to place the words that sound the same in groups and then to explain the meaning of each word.

Idea Bookmarks: For this activity, students take reflective notes from the books they are reading on bookmark-size pieces of paper. The bookmarks include quotes, observations, and words that strike the reader as interesting or effective. The bookmarks can be divided into boxes to add more quotes and page numbers (Samway, 2006).

IEPT (Inter-Ethno-linguistic Peer Tutoring): This research-based method increases fluency for English Learners by pairing them with fluent English speakers. In highly-structured tasks, fluent English speakers are trained to promote extensive interaction with English Learners.

Improv Read Aloud: During this exercise, students act out a story silently while the teacher or another student reads it aloud. Each student has a role to play and has to improvise the part while the story is being read. Afterward, students discuss the techniques and ideas students used to act out their part during the improv (Zwiers, 2008).

Insert Method: In this activity, students read text with a partner and mark the texts with the following coding system: a check to show a concept or fact already known, a question mark to show a concept that is confusing, an exclamation mark to show something new or surprising, or a plus to show an idea or concept that is new (Echevarria, Vogt, & Short, 2017).

Inside/Outside Circle: Students form two concentric circles facing one another, an inside circle and an outside circle. Students can then participate in a short, guided discussion or review with their partner. After the discussion, the outside circle rotates one person to the right while the inside circle remains still. All students now have a new partner. This exercise facilitates student conversations (Kagan, 1990).

Instructional Conversation: During this activity, students engage in conversation about literature through open-ended dialogue with the teacher or with students in small groups. Instructional conversations have few "known answer" questions; therefore they promote complex language and expression (Goldenberg, 1992).

Instructional Scaffolding: This model of teaching helps students achieve increasing levels of independence following the pattern: teach, model, practice, and apply (Echevarria, Vogt, & Short, 2017).

Interactive Reading Logs: Reading logs are used by students during silent reading to reflect on the text. These logs can be exchanged with other students or with the teacher for questions, comments, or responses. These logs are ideal components of an SSR program.

Interview Grids: Interview grids help students record other student's responses to various questions that express: facts, opinions, perspectives, analyses, suggestions, and hypotheses. To engage in this activity, students interview a partner in the classroom who responds to their list of questions (Zwiers, 2008).

For example:

	Why are there waves in the ocean?	Why do you think some waves are higher than others?
BRIAN		
ENRIQUE		
CHRISTINA		

Keep, Delete, Substitute, Select: Students learn a strategy for summarizing developed by Brown, Campoine, and Day (1981) as discussed in Classroom Instruction That Works (Marzano, Pickering, & Pollock, 2001). When using this strategy, students keep important information, delete unnecessary and redundant material, substitute general terms for specific terms (e.g. birds for robins or crows, etc.), and select or create a topic sentence. For ELs, Hill and Flynn (2006) recommend using gestures to represent each phase of the process and to explain the difference between high frequency and low frequency terms.

KID (Keyword, Information, Drawing): In this activity, students list a word, important information about the word, and then a drawing of the word.

KIM (Key, Information, Memory Cue) Chart: This graphic organizer lets students organize what they are learning, have learned, or need to review. In the K (Key) section of the organizer, students jot down key points that are being taught or that have been learned. In the I (Information) section, students list important information that supports those points. And in the M (Memory Cue) section, students create a visual representation as a summary of what was learned (Castillo, 2012).

KWL (Know/Want to Know/Learned): This is a pre-reading strategy used to access prior knowledge and set up new learning experiences (Ogle, 1986). To begin, the teacher creates a chart where students respond to three questions: What do you know? What do you want to know? What have you learned? The first two questions are discussed prior to reading, and the third is discussed after reading. When discussing the third question, students may find they have changed their minds based on information they gathered while reading.

Language Proficiency Level: This is a measure of a student's ability to listen, speak, read, and write in English.

Learning Logs and Journals: Students can record observations and questions about what they are learning in a particular content area with learning logs or journals. The teacher can provide general or specific sentence starters to help students reflect on their learning (Samway, 2006).

Letters/Editorials: For this activity, students can write letters and editorials from their own point of view or from the point of view of a character in a novel, a person from history, or a physical object (sun, atom, frog, etc.). Teachers of ELs should remember to scaffold the writing process by providing sentence frames, graphic organizers, wordlists, and other writing supports. Newcomers may use the Draw & Write method (see explanation above).

Linguistic Accommodations: The ways to provide access to curriculum and opportunities for language development for English Learners are: comprehensible input, differentiating based on language proficiency level, and scaffolding.

List/Group/Label: Students are given a list of words or students brainstorm a list of words as they engage in listing, grouping, and labeling. They sort the words on this list into similar piles and create labels for each pile. This can be done by topic (planets, stars, scientific laws, etc.) or by word type (those beginning with a particular letter, those with a particular suffix, or those in a particular tense) (Taba, 1967).

List Stressed Words: Students take a written paragraph and highlight words that would be stressed, focusing on stressing content English words such as nouns, verbs, adverbs over process words such as articles, prepositions, linking-verbs/modals and auxiliaries.

Literacy: To be literate, students have to have the ability to use and process printed and written material in a specific affective filter.

Literature Circles: In this activity students form small groups similar to "book clubs" to discuss literature. Roles include: discussion facilitators, passage pickers, illustrators, connectors, summarizers, vocabulary enrichers, travel tracers, investigators, and figurative language finders. ELs will need to be supported with sentence starters, wordlists, and adapted text as necessary, depending on language level (Schlick & Johnson, 1999). For support in starting literature circles see: www.litcircles.org

Margin Notes: This is a way of adapting text. Teachers, students, or volunteers write key terms, translations of key terms, short native language summaries, text clarifications, or hints for understanding in the margins of a textbook (Echevarria, Vogt, & Short, 2017).

Math Sorts: This sorting activity requires that students classify numbers, equations, geometric shapes, etc. based on given categories. For example, students are given twenty systems of linear equations cards and they have to determine whether each system belongs in the category of parallel lines, perpendicular lines, or neither.

Mix and Match: This activity encourages students to interact with classmates and to practice formal and informal English. To begin, each student is given a card that has information matching another student's card. When the teacher says, "Mix," students stand and walk around the room. When the teacher says, "Match," students find their match by using the sentence stem, "I have _____. Who has _____?"

Mortar Words: Mortar words are general academic words that can be found in textbooks, tests, and conversations across all subject areas. Mortar words hold academic language (i.e., specific technical words/terms) together in a sentence. They include transitional words like because, signal words like first or second, and test-specific language like best represents or based upon. Mortar words are often abstract, and without a clear definition, so the best way for students to learn these words is by using them. Mortar words allow students to put complex and formal structures together when communicating.

Multiple Representations Card Game: This activity is a variation of the Spoons card game. Depending on the number of cards, students play in groups of 3-5. The objective of the game is to be the first player to get all the representations of a particular math concept.

Multiple Representations Graphic Organizer (MRGO): This is an instructional tool used to illustrate an algebraic situation in multiple representations that could include: pictures, graphs, tables, equations, or verbal descriptions (Echevarria, Vogt, & Short, 2017).

Native Language Brainstorm: This method allows students to think about and list ideas related to a concept in their native language.

Native Language Texts: Native language translations, chapter summaries, word lists, glossaries, or related literature can be used to understand texts from content-area classes. Many textbook companies include Spanish language resources with textbook adoption.

Nonlinguistic Representations: Nonlinguistic means of representing knowledge include illustrations, graphic organizers, physical models, and kinesthetic activities. Marzano, Pickering, and Pollock (2001) and Hill and Flynn (2006) advocate integrating Total Physical Response (Asher, 1969) with nonlinguistic representations to engage learners in the early stages of language development.

Note-Taking Strategies: Students learn strategies for organizing information presented in lectures and in texts during note-taking. English Learners, at the early stages of language development, benefit from Guided Notes (see description above), native language wordlists, summaries, and opportunities to clarify concepts with peers. Strategies include informal outlines, concept webbing, Cornell Note-taking, and combination notes (see descriptions above). Research indicates that students should write more, rather than less, when taking notes (Marzano, Pickering, & Pollock, 2001). ELs in pre-production phases can respond to teacher notes through gestures. Those in early production and speech emergent phases can communicate using teacher provided sentence frames (Hill & Flynn, 2006).

Numbered Heads Together: This strategy enables all students, in small groups, a chance to share with the whole class. Each student in a group is assigned a number (1, 2, 3, and 4). When asking questions, the teacher will ask all the Ones to speak first, and then open the discussion to the rest of the class. For the next question, the teacher will ask the Twos to speak, then the Threes, and finally the Fours. The teacher can also randomize which number will speak in which order. When doing numbered heads with English Learners, teachers should provide sentence starters for the students (Kagan, 1992).

Oral Scaffolding: This is the process of: teaching academic language explicitly, modeling academic language, providing structured opportunities to use academic language in oral expression, and writing with academic language (Adapted from Gibbons, 2002).

Order It Up Math Puzzle: In this activity, a number sentence or equation is written on a sentence strip. The sentence strip is cut into individual pieces and placed in an envelope. Students work in pairs to determine the correct order of each piece and to come up with the original number sentence/equation (Created by Amy King, Independent Consultant).

Outlines: This traditional note-taking method makes use of Roman numerals, Arabic numerals, and upper/lowercase letters.

Pairs View: When watching a video clip or movie, each pair of students is assigned a role. For example, one partner might be responsible for identifying key dates while another is listing important people and their actions (Kagan, 1992). This strategy keeps students engaged and focused while they process information.

Paragraph Frames: Incomplete paragraphs provide scaffolds for language development by offering opportunities to develop academic writing and communication skills.

Partner Reading: This strategy for processing text requires two students to read a text. While reading, readers alternate paragraphs, allowing one student to summarize while the other student reads and vice versa (Johnson & Johnson, 1995).

Peer Editing: During this activity, students review one another's work using a rubric. Research shows that English Learners benefit from peer editing when trained using peer response strategies (Berg, 1999).

PERSIAN: This acronym is used to analyze the characteristics of a society. Elements include: political, economic, religious, social, intellectual, artistic, and near. This framework helps organize thinking about history.

Personal Dictionary: To engage in this activity, students choose words from the word wall, wordlists, or words encountered in texts. Words are recorded on note cards or in notebooks, which become personal dictionaries. Students are encouraged to draw, reflect, or use their native language when writing definitions (Adapted from Echevarria, Vogt, & Short, 2017).

Personal Spelling Guide: On note cards, students record correct spellings of misspelled words from their writing. As the number of cards grows, students can sort the words, based on each word's characteristics. For example, students can generate categories such as: contractions, big words, words with "ie" or "ei," words that are hard to say, words I have never used, etc. Encourage students to look for spelling patterns as they make lists. To assess spelling knowledge, students can choose a number of self-selected words and have a partner quiz them orally.

Perspective-Based Writing: This activity requires students to write from an assigned point of view using specific academic language. For example, students in a social studies class could write from the perspective of Martin Luther King, Jr., explaining his participation in the Montgomery bus boycott to a fellow pastor. As part of this activity, students are given specific words and phrases to integrate into the writing assignment. Students can also write from the point of view of inanimate objects such as rocks, water, molecules, etc. and describe processes from an imaginative perspective. In addition, students can take on the role of an expert within a field: math, science, social studies, or literature, and use the language of the discipline to write about a particular topic. Genre studies can be a particularly helpful way of preparing students for perspective-based writing activities (Seidlitz & Perryman, 2011).

Polya's Problem-Solving Method: This is a four-step model for solving word problems.
• Step 1: Understanding the problem
• Step 2: Devising a plan
• Step 3: Carrying out the plan
• Step 4: Check

Posted Phrases and Stems: Sentence frames posted in clearly visible locations in the classroom give students easy access to functional language during writing tasks. For example, during a lab, the teacher might post the following sentence stems: "How do I record….," "Can you help me gather/ mix/measure/ identify/list….," "Can you explain what you mean by …?" Sentence stems should be posted in English but can be written in the native language as well.

Prediction Café: This activity is a way for students to participate in mini-discussions about prediction. Pick out important headings, quotations, or captions from a text (about eight quotations for a class of 24) and write them on cards. Have students read/discuss what they think the text might be about or what they think will happen in the text, based on the information on the card. (Note: Even though some students may receive the same card, predictions will vary.) Students should be given frames to facilitate the development of academic language during the activity such as: " __makes me think that..," "I believe ___ because…," etc.) (Zwiers, 2008).

Pretest with a Partner: In pairs, students are given a pretest. Students take turns reading the questions, and after each question they try to come to consensus on answers. This activity prepares students for a unit of study (Echevarria, Vogt, & Short, 2017).

Question Answer Relationship (QAR): This is a way of teaching students to analyze the nature of questions they are asked about a text (Echevarria, Vogt, & Short, 2017). Questions are divided into four categories:

• Right there (found in the text)

• Think and Search (requires thinking about relationships between ideas in the text)

• Author and Me (requires making an inference about the text)

• On My Own (requires reflection on experience and knowledge)

Question the Author (QtA): This is a strategy for deepening the level of thinking about literature (Beck, McKeown, Hamilton, & Kugan, 1997). Instead of staying within the realm of the text, the teacher prompts students to think about the author's purpose. For example:

• What do you think the author is trying to say?

• Why do you think the author chose that word or phrase?

• Would you have chosen a different word or phrase?

Question, Signal, Stem, Share, Assess: This strategy helps students use new academic language during student-student interactions. The teacher asks a question and then asks students to give a signal when they are ready to share their responses with another student. To respond, students must use a particular sentence stem provided by the teacher. Students are then assessed orally or in writing (Seidlitz & Perryman, 2011).

Quick Write: Within a short time period, students are asked to respond in writing to a specific content concept.

Radio Talk Show: Students create a radio talk show about a particular topic. This can be a good opportunity for students to practice using academic language as they take on the role of an expert. It also provides an opportunity for students to identify the differences between formal and informal use of English as they play different roles (Wilhelm, 2002).

R.A.F.T. (Role/Audience/Format/Topic): This Social Studies writing strategy enables students to write from various points of view (Fisher & Frey, 2007). The letters stand for Role (the perspective the students take); Audience (the individuals the author is addressing); Format (the type of writing that will take place); and Topic (the subject).

Read, Write, Pair, Share: This strategy encourages students to share their writing and ideas during interactions. Students read a text, write their thoughts using a sentence starter, pair with another student, and share their writing. Students can also be given suggestions about responding to one another's writing (Fisher & Frey, 2007).

Reader/Writer/Speaker Response Triads: This is a way of processing text in cooperative groups. To begin, students form groups of three. One student reads the text aloud; one writes the group's reactions or responses to questions about the text, a third reports the answers to the group. After reporting to the group, the students switch roles (Echevarria, Vogt, & Short, 2017).

Recasting: For this activity, repeat an English Learner's incorrect statement or question correctly. Do not change the meaning or the low-risk environment. Be sure the learner feels comfortable during the interaction. Recasts have been shown to have a positive impact on second language acquisition (Leeman, 2003).

Reciprocal Teaching: Reciprocal teaching requires a student leader to guide the class through the following learning stages: Summarizing, Question Generating, Clarifying, and Predicting. This student-student interaction involves collaboration to create meaning from texts. Palincsar and Brown (1985) and Hill and Flynn (2006) suggest adapting reciprocal teaching for use among English Learners by providing vocabulary, modeling language use, and using pictorial representation during the discussion.

Related Literature: Related literature is text that connects and supports subject-area content. These texts can be fiction or nonfiction, in the native language, or in the target language (Echevarria, Vogt, & Short, 2017).

ReQuest: This is a variation of reciprocal teaching (see description above). The teacher asks questions using particular sentence stems after a SSR session (see description below). During the next SSR session, the teacher provides stems for students to use when responding to the text (Manzo, 1969, as cited in Fisher & Frey, 2007).

Retelling: During this activity, students retell a narrative text or summarize an expository text using their own words.

Roundtable: This is a cooperative learning technique in which small groups are given a paper with a category, term, or task listed. The paper is passed around the table and each group member is responsible for writing a characteristic, synonym, step, or task that represents the category, term, or task (Kagan, 1992).

Same Scene Twice: Students perform a skit that involves individuals discussing a given topic. The first time, the individuals are novices who use informal language to discuss the topic. The second time, they are experts who discuss the topic using correct academic terminology and academic English (Adapted from Wilhelm, 2002).

Scanning: Students scan through a text backwards looking for unfamiliar terms. The teacher then provides quick, brief definitions for the terms, giving only the meaning of the word as it appears in context. Marzano, Pickering, and Pollock (2001) state that "even superficial instruction on words greatly enhances the probability that students will learn the words from context when they encounter them during reading," and that, "the effects of vocabulary instruction are even more powerful when the words selected are those that students will most likely encounter when they learn new content."

Sculptorades: Based on one of the tasks in the board game Cranium, this strategy requires each student to use sculpting clay to represent a concept, object, organism, or process. Students can be assigned a broad category or given specific vocabulary terms to model. All students should sculpt at the same time, preferably behind folders. One at a time, each student reveals their sculpture, and the other group members try to determine what the sculpture represents.

Segmental Practice: These listening/discriminating activities help English Learners listen for and practice pronouncing individual combinations of syllables. There are several ways to engage in segmental practice. Tongue Twisters and comparisons with native language pronunciations help English Learners practice English pronunciation. Using "syllable, storm, say," students brainstorm syllables that begin with a particular sound, e.g., pat, pen, pal, pas, pon, pem, etc. Long and short vowel sounds can be used as well as diphthongs. Students can practice with partners (Celce-Murcia, Brinton, & Goodwin, 1996, as cited in Florez, M. 1998).

Self-Assessment of Levels of Word Knowledge: Students rank their knowledge of new words on the word wall and other word lists using total response signals (see description below) or sentence starters. Responses range from no familiarity with the word to understanding a word well enough to explain it to others (Diamond & Gutlohn, 2006, as cited in Echevarria, Vogt, & Short, 2017).

Sentence Frames: Incomplete sentences provide the opportunity to scaffold language development structures that help students develop academic language.

Sentence Mark Up: Students use colored pencils to mark texts for cause and effect, opposing thoughts, connecting words, and other features of sentences. This strategy helps students understand the relationship between clauses (Zwiers, 2008).

Sentence Sort: This activity requires students to sort various sentences based on characteristics. The teacher provides the sentences, and the students sort them. In an "open sort," students create the categories; in a "closed sort," teachers create the categories. Sentences can also be taken from a paragraph in a textbook or from class literature.

Possible categories include:

• Descriptive sentences
• Complex sentences
• Simple sentences
• Sentences connecting ideas
• Sentences comparing ideas
• Sentences opposing ideas
• Sentences with correct usage
• Sentences with incorrect usage
• Sentences in formal English
• Sentences in informal English

Sentence Stems: Incomplete sentences are provided to scaffold the development of specific language structures and to facilitate entry into conversation and writing. For example, "In my opinion..." or "One characteristic of annelids is..."

Signal Words: Signal words determine a text pattern such as generalization, cause and effect, process, sequence, etc.

A sample of signal words can be found at: www.lincs.ed.gov/ readingprofiles/Signal_Words.pdf

Six-Step Vocabulary Process: This research-based process, developed by Marzano (2004), helps teachers take different steps to build student academic vocabulary. The steps are: Teacher provides a description of a vocabulary word/term. Students restate the description in their own words. Students create a nonlinguistic representation of the word/term. Students periodically do activities that help them add to their knowledge of vocabulary words/terms. Periodically, students are asked to discuss the terms with each other. Periodically, students are involved in games that allow them to "play" with the terms.

SOAPST (Speaker/Occasion/Audience/Purpose/Subject/ Tone): This AP writing strategy requires students to address a speaker, occasion, audience, subject, or tone using narrative, persuasive, or analytical writing styles (Morse, 2011).

Social Language: This is informal language that students use in relationships with peers, friends, and family.

Songs, Poems, Rhymes: Teachers use songs, poems, and rhymes for the purpose of practicing social studies words/ terms in the classroom.

Sound Scripting: This is a way for students to mark text showing pauses and stress. Students write a paragraph, enter a paragraph break to show pauses, and use capital and bold letters to show word stress (Powell, 1996).

SQP2RS (Squeepers): This classroom reading strategy trains students to use cognitive/metacognitive strategies to process nonfiction text (Echevarria, Vogt, & Short, 2017). The following steps are involved:

• Survey: Students scan the visuals, headings, and other text features.

• Question: Students write a list of questions they might answer while reading.

• Predict: Students write predictions about what they will learn.

- Read: Students read the text.

- Respond: Students revisit their questions and think through responses to reading.

SSR Program (Sustained, Silent Reading Program): This program encourages students to read books of their choice during a silent reading period of 15-20 minutes per day. Pilgreen (2000) defines the eight features of high-quality SSR programs as: access to books, book appeal, conducive reading environment, encouragement to read, non-account-ability, distributed reading time, staff training, and follow up activities.

Story Telling: In this activity, students retell narratives in their native language.

Structured Academic Controversy: This is a way of structuring classroom discussion to promote deep thinking and to understand multiple perspectives. Johnson & Johnson (1995) outline these five steps:

- Organizing information and deriving conclusions

- Presenting and advocating positions

- Uncertainty created by being challenged by opposing views

- Epistemic curiosity and perspective taking

- Re-conceptualizing, synthesizing, and integrating

Structured Conversation: In this activity, student/student interaction is explicitly planned. Students are given sentence frames to begin the conversation as well as specific questions and sentence starters for the purpose of elaboration.

Summarization Frames: This is a way of structuring summaries of content area text. The frames involve specific questions that help students summarize different kinds of texts. Marzano et al. (2001) and Hill and Flynn (2006) discuss seven frames:

- narrative frame
- topic restriction frame
- illustration frame
- definition frame
- argumentation frame
- problem solution frame
- conversation frame

Supra-segmental Practice: This activity involves pronunciation practice with groups of syllables. Some techniques include: sound scripting, recasting, pronunciation portfolio, and content/function word comparisons (Wennerstrom, 1993).

Systematic Phonics Instruction: This method teaches sound/spelling relationships and how to use those relationships to read. The National Literacy Panel (August & Shanahan, 2006) reported that instruction in phonemic awareness, phonics, and fluency had "clear benefits for language minority students."

T-Chart, Pair, Defend: On a T-Chart, students write evidence to support two opposing points of view. In pairs, students take turns arguing from each point of view.

Taped Text: Recordings of text can be used as a way of adapting text for English Learners (Echevarria, Vogt, & Short, 2017).

Think-Alouds: Thinking aloud allows teachers to scaffold cognitive and metacognitive thinking by verbalizing the thought process (Bauman, Jones, & Seifert-Kessell, 1993).

Think, Pair, Share: This method encourages student/student interaction. The teacher asks a question and then provides wait time. The students then find a partner and compare their answers. Afterward, selected students share their thoughts with the whole class (Lyman, 1981).

Ticket Out: To get a "Ticket Out" of class, students write a short reflection at the end of a lesson. The reflection includes facts, details, ideas, impressions, opinions, information, and vocabulary from the unit they have just studied. To help students begin writing a prompt can be offered.

Tiered Questions: In this activity, there are various types of questions for students that are based on individual levels of language development (Hill & Flynn, 2006).

Tiered Response Stems: This activity asks a single question but allows students to choose from a variety of stems to construct responses. When responding, students can use a sentence stem based on their level of language knowledge and proficiency (Seidlitz & Perryman, 2011).

Total Physical Response (TPR): This is a way of teaching that uses gesture and movement to make content comprehensible to ESL newcomers (Asher, 1969).

Total Response Signals (also called Active Response Signals): Total response signals, such as thumbs up/down, white boards, and response cards, can be used by students when responding to questions. Response signals show levels of comprehension instantly.

Unit Study for English Learners: This modified approach to Writers' Workshop is advocated by Samway (2006). The steps involve:

• Gathering high quality samples of a genre

• Immersion in books

• Sifting between books that students can model and those they can't

• Repetitive immersion/second reading of the books

• Imitating writing techniques found in published writing

• Writing and publishing

• Reflecting and assessing

Visual Literacy Frames: This is a framework for improving visual literacy focusing on affective, compositional, and critical dimensions of visual information processing (Callow, 2008).

Visuals: Illustrations, graphic organizers, manipulatives, models, and real world objects are used to make content comprehensible for English Learners.

Vocabulary Alive: Students memorize a lesson's key vocabulary by applying gestures to each term. The gestures can be assigned by the teacher or by students. Once the gestures are determined, each term and its gesture is introduced by saying, "The word is _____ , and it looks like this ____" (Created by Cristina Ferrari, Brownsville ISD).

Vocabulary Game Shows: Using games like Jeopardy, Pictionary, and Who Wants to be a Millionaire, etc., allows students a chance to practice academic vocabulary.

Vocabulary Self-Collection Strategy (VSS): This is a research-based method of vocabulary instruction involving student collection of words for class study. As students share their lists, they tell: where the word was found, the definition of the word, and why the class should study that particular word (Ruddell & Shearer, 2002).

W.I.T. Questioning: This is a questioning strategy that trains students to use three stems to promote elaboration during discussion (Seidlitz & Perryman, 2011):

• Why do you think...?

• Is there another...?

• Tell me more about...

Whip Around: This is a way of getting input from all students during a class discussion (Fisher & Frey, 2007). To begin, the teacher asks students to write a bulleted list in response to an open-ended question. Students write their responses to the question and then stand up. The teacher calls on students, one at a time, to respond to the question. If students have the same answer as the student who is responding, they cross it off their lists. The teacher continues to call on students for responses, and students continue to cross off answers that are similar. When all answers have been deleted, the students sit down. The activity concludes when all students are seated.

Word Analysis: In this activity, students study the parts, origins, and structures of words for the purpose of improving spelling skills (Harrington, 1996).

Word Generation: In this activity, students brainstorm words having particular roots. Teachers then have students predict the meaning of the word based on the roots (Echevarria, Vogt, & Short, 2017).

Word, Model, Expand, and Sound Questioning (WMES Questioning): This is a method of differentiating instruction developed by Hill and Flynn (2006). The mnemonic device stands for "Word, Model, Expand, and Sound."

• Word: Teachers work on word selection with pre-production students.

• Model: Teachers model for early production.

• Expand: Teachers expand the written or spoken language of speech emergent students.

• Sound: Teachers help intermediate and advanced fluency students sound "like a book" by working on fluency.

Word Play: In this activity, students manipulate words through various word games designed to increase understanding. Schlick Noe and Johnson (1999) divide word games into eight categories: onomastics (name games), expressions, figures of speech, word associations, word formations, word manipulations, word games, and ambiguities.

Word Sorts: Sorting words based on structure and spelling can improve orthography (Bear et al., 2000).

Word Splash: Select key vocabulary words or words connected to a concept and write them for students to see. Tell students you wrote the words in no particular order (called a splash). Have students begin to categorize the words in some logical order. Ask students to choose the words from one category to use in a written paragraph, and then ask them to share it orally with the class.

Word Study Books: In this activity, students organize words in a notebook based on spelling, affixes, and roots (Bear et al., 2000).

Word Walls: Word walls are a collection of words posted on a classroom wall used to improve literacy. Not only do they become silent teachers that remind students of words studied in class, but they provide opportunities to have language moments whenever possible. Word walls can be organized by topic, sound, or spelling. The content on word walls should be changed as units of study are completed (Eyraud et al., 2000).

Written Conversation: Using planned language and content, students interact during writing conversation. To complete this activity, students work in pairs as they respond to questions and sentence starters provided by the teacher.

§74.4. English Language Proficiency Standards

(a) Introduction.

(1) The English language proficiency standards in this section outline English language proficiency level descriptors and student expectations for English language learners (ELs). School districts shall implement this section as an integral part of each subject in the required curriculum. The English language proficiency standards are to be published along with the Texas Essential Knowledge and Skills (TEKS) for each subject in the required curriculum.

(2) In order for ELs to be successful, they must acquire both social and academic language proficiency in English. Social language proficiency in English consists of the English needed for daily social interactions. Academic language proficiency consists of the English needed to think critically, understand and learn new concepts, process complex academic material, and interact and communicate in English academic settings.

(3) Classroom instruction that effectively integrates second language acquisition with quality content area instruction ensures that ELs acquire social and academic language proficiency in English, learn the knowledge and skills in the TEKS, and reach their full academic potential.

(4) Effective instruction in second language acquisition involves giving ELs opportunities to listen, speak, read, and write at their current levels of English development while gradually increasing the linguistic complexity of the English they read and hear, and are expected to speak and write.

(5) The cross-curricular second language acquisition skills in subsection (c) of this section apply to ELLs in Kindergarten–Grade 12.

(6) The English language proficiency levels of beginning, intermediate, advanced, and advanced high are not grade-specific. ELs may exhibit different proficiency levels within the language domains of listening, speaking, reading, and writing. The proficiency level descrip-tors outlined in subsection (d) of this section show the progression of second language acquisition from one proficiency level to the next and serve as a road map to help content area teachers instruct ELLs commensurate with students' linguistic needs.

(b) School district responsibilities. In fulfilling the requirements of this section, school districts shall:

(1) identify the student's English language proficiency levels in the domains of listening, speaking, reading, and writing in accordance with the proficiency level descriptors for the beginning, intermediate, advanced, and advanced high levels delineated in subsection (d) of this section;

(2) provide instruction in the knowledge and skills of the foundation and enrichment curriculum in a manner that is linguistically accommodated (communicated, sequenced, and scaffolded) commensurate with the student's levels of English language proficiency to ensure that the student learns the knowledge and skills in the required curriculum;

(3) provide content-based instruction including the cross-curricular second language acquisition essential knowledge and skills in subsection (c) of this section in a manner that is linguistically accommodated to help the student acquire English language proficiency; and

(4) provide intensive and ongoing foundational second language acquisition instruction to ELLs in Grade 3 or higher who are at the beginning or intermediate level of English language proficiency in listening, speaking, reading, and/or writing as determined by the state's English language proficiency assessment system. These ELs require focused, targeted, and systematic second language acquisition instruction to provide them with the foundation of English language vocabulary, grammar, syntax, and English mechanics necessary to support content-based instruction and accelerated learning of English.

(c) Cross-curricular second language acquisition essential knowledge and skills.

(1) Cross-curricular second language acquisition/ learning strategies. The ELL uses language learning strategies to develop an awareness of his or her own learning processes in all content areas. In order for the EL to meet grade-level learning expectations across the foundation and enrichment curriculum, all instruction delivered in English must be linguistically accommodated (communicated, sequenced, and scaffolded) commensurate with the student's level of English language proficiency. The student is expected to:

(A) use prior knowledge and experiences to understand meanings in English;

(B) monitor oral and written language production and employ self-corrective techniques or other resources;

(C) use strategic learning techniques such as concept mapping, drawing, memorizing, comparing, contrasting, and reviewing to acquire basic and grade-level vocabulary;

(D) speak using learning strategies such as requesting assistance, employing non-verbal cues, and using synonyms and circumlocution (conveying ideas by defining or describing when exact English words are not known);

(E) internalize new basic and academic language by using and reusing it in meaningful ways in speaking and writing activities that build concept and language attainment;

(F) use accessible language and learn new and essential language in the process;

(G) demonstrate an increasing ability to distinguish between formal and informal English and an increasing knowledge of when to use each one commensurate with grade-level learning expectations; and

(H) develop and expand repertoire of learning strategies such as reasoning inductively or deductively, looking for patterns in language, and analyzing sayings and expressions commensurate with grade-level learning expectations.

(2) Cross-curricular second language acquisition/ listening. The ELL listens to a variety of speakers including teachers, peers, and electronic media to gain an increasing level of comprehension of newly acquired language in all content areas. L may be at the beginning, intermediate, advanced, or advanced high stage of English language acquisition in listening. In order for the EL to meet grade-level learning expectations across the foundation and enrichment curriculum, all instruction delivered in English must be linguistically accommodated (communicated, sequenced, and scaffolded) commensurate with the student's level of English language proficiency. The student is expected to:

(A) distinguish sounds and intonation patterns of English with increasing ease;

(B) recognize elements of the English sound system in newly acquired vocabulary such as long and short vowels, silent letters, and consonant clusters;

(C) learn new language structures, expressions, and basic and academic vocabulary heard during classroom instruction and interactions;

(D) monitor understanding of spoken language during classroom instruction and interactions and seek clarification as needed;

(E) use visual, contextual, and linguistic support to enhance and confirm understanding of increasingly complex and elaborated spoken language;

(F) listen to and derive meaning from a variety of media such as audio tape, video, DVD, and CD ROM to build and reinforce concept and language attainment;

(G) understand the general meaning, main points, and important details of spoken language ranging from situations in which topics, language, and contexts are familiar to unfamiliar;

(H) understand implicit ideas and information in increasingly complex spoken language commensurate with grade-level learning expectations; and

(I) demonstrate listening comprehension of increasingly complex spoken English by following directions, retelling or summarizing spoken messages, responding to questions and requests, collaborating with peers, and taking notes commensurate with content and grade-level needs.

(3) Cross-curricular second language acquisition/speaking. The EL speaks in a variety of modes for a variety of purposes with an awareness of different language registers (formal/informal) using vocabulary with increasing fluency and accuracy in language arts and all content areas. ELs may be at the beginning, intermediate, advanced, or advanced high stage of English language acquisition in speaking. In order for the EL to meet grade-level learning expectations across the foundation and enrichment curriculum, all instruction delivered in English must be linguistically accommodated (communicated, sequenced, and scaffolded) commensurate with the student's level of English language proficiency. The student is expected to:

(A) practice producing sounds of newly acquired vocabulary such as long and short vowels, silent letters, and consonant clusters to pronounce English words in a manner that is increasingly comprehensible;

(B) expand and internalize initial English vocabulary by learning and using high-frequency English words necessary for identifying and describing people, places, and objects, by retelling simple stories and basic information represented or supported by pictures, and by learning and using routine language needed for classroom communication;

(C) speak using a variety of grammatical structures, sentence lengths, sentence types, and connecting words with increasing accuracy and ease as more English is acquired;

(D) speak using grade-level content area vocabulary in context to internalize new English words and build academic language proficiency;

(E) share information in cooperative learning interactions;

(F) ask and give information ranging from using a very limited bank of high-frequency, high-need, concrete vocabulary, including key words and expressions needed for basic communication in academic and social contexts, to using abstract and content-based vocabulary during extended speaking assignments;

(G) express opinions, ideas, and feelings ranging from communicating single words and short phrases to participating in extended discussions on a variety of social and grade-appropriate academic topics;

(H) narrate, describe, and explain with increasing specificity and detail as more English is acquired;

(I) adapt spoken language appropriately for formal and informal purposes; and

(J) respond orally to information presented in a wide variety of print, electronic, audio, and visual media to build and reinforce concept and language attainment.

(4) Cross-curricular second language acquisition/reading. The EL reads a variety of texts for a variety of purposes with an increasing level of comprehension in all content areas. ELs may be at the beginning, intermediate, advanced, or advanced high stage of English language acquisition in reading. In order for the EL to meet grade-level learning expectations across the foundation and enrichment curriculum, all instruction delivered in English must be linguistically accommodated (communicated, sequenced, and scaffolded) commensurate with the student's level of English language proficiency. For Kindergarten and Grade 1, certain of these student expectations apply to text read aloud for students not yet at the stage of decoding written text. The student is expected to:

(A) learn relationships between sounds and letters of the English language and decode (sound out) words using a combination of skills such as recognizing sound–letter relationships and identifying cognates, affixes, roots, and base words;

(B) recognize directionality of English reading such as left to right and top to bottom;

(C) develop basic sight vocabulary, derive meaning of environmental print, and comprehend English vocabulary and language structures used routinely in written classroom materials;

(D) use prereading supports such as graphic organizers, illustrations, and pretaught topic-related vocabulary and other prereading activities to enhance comprehension of written text;

(E) read linguistically accommodated content area material with a decreasing need for linguistic accommodations as more English is learned;

(F) use visual and contextual support and support from peers and teachers to read grade-appropriate content area text, enhance and confirm understanding, and develop vocabulary, grasp of language structures, and background knowledge needed to comprehend increasingly challenging language;

(G) demonstrate comprehension of increasingly complex English by participating in shared reading, retelling or summarizing material, responding to questions, and taking notes commensurate with content area and grade-level needs;

(H) read silently with increasing ease and comprehension for longer periods;

(I) demonstrate English comprehension and expand reading skills by employing basic reading skills such as demonstrating understanding of supporting ideas and details in text and graphic sources, summarizing text, and distinguishing main ideas from details commensurate with content area needs;

(J) demonstrate English comprehension and expand reading skills by employing inferential skills such as predicting, making connections between ideas, drawing inferences and conclusions from text and graphic sources, and finding supporting text evidence commensurate with content area needs; and

(K) demonstrate English comprehension and expand reading skills by employing analytical skills such as evaluating written information and performing critical analyses commensurate with content area and grade-level needs.

(5) Cross-curricular second language acquisition/writing. The ELL writes in a variety of forms with increasing accuracy to effectively address a specific purpose and audience in all content areas. ELs may be at the beginning, intermediate, advanced, or advanced high stage of English language acquisition in writing. In order for the EL to meet grade-level learning expectations across foundation and enrichment curriculum, all instruction delivered in English must be linguistically accommodated (communicated, sequenced, and scaffolded) commensurate with the student's level of English language proficiency. For Kindergarten and Grade 1, certain of these student expectations do not apply until the student has reached the stage of generating original written text using a standard writing system. The student is expected to:

(A) learn relationships between sounds and letters of the English language to represent sounds when writing in English;

(B) write using newly acquired basic vocabulary and content-based grade-level vocabulary;

(C) spell familiar English words with increasing accuracy, and employ English spelling patterns and rules with increasing accuracy as more English is acquired;

(D) edit writing for standard grammar and usage, including subject-verb agreement, pronoun agreement, and appropriate verb tenses commensurate with grade-level expectations as more English is acquired;

(E) employ increasingly complex grammatical structures in content area writing commensurate with grade-level expectations, such as:

(i) using correct verbs, tenses, and pronouns/antecedents;

(ii) using possessive case (apostrophe s) correctly; and

(iii) using negatives and contractions correctly;

(F) write using a variety of grade-appropriate sentence lengths, patterns, and connecting words to combine phrases, clauses, and sentences in increasingly accurate ways as more English is acquired; and

(G) narrate, describe, and explain with increasing specificity and detail to fulfill content area writing needs as more English is acquired.

(d) Proficiency level descriptors.

(1) Listening, Kindergarten-Grade 12. ELLs may be at the beginning, intermediate, advanced, or advanced high stage of English language acquisition in listening. The following proficiency level descriptors for listening are sufficient to describe the overall English language proficiency levels of ELs in this language domain in order to linguistically accommodate their instruction.

(A) Beginning. Beginning ELs have little or no ability to understand spoken English in academic and social settings. These students:

(i) struggle to understand simple conversations and simple discussions even when the topics are familiar and the speaker uses linguistic supports such as visuals, slower speech and other verbal cues, and gestures;

(ii) struggle to identify and distinguish individual words and phrases during social and instructional interactions that have not been intentionally modified for ELs; and

(iii) may not seek clarification in English when failing to comprehend the English they hear; frequently remain silent, watching others for cues.

(B) Intermediate. Intermediate ELs have the ability to understand simple, high-frequency spoken English used in routine academic and social settings. These students:

(i) usually understand simple or routine directions, as well as short, simple conversations and short, simple discussions on familiar topics; when topics are unfamiliar, require extensive linguistic supports and adaptations such as visuals, slower speech and other verbal cues, simplified language, gestures, and preteaching to preview or build topic-related vocabulary;

(ii) often identify and distinguish key words and phrases necessary to understand the general meaning during social and basic instructional interactions that have not been intentionally modified for ELs; and

(iii) have the ability to seek clarification in English when failing to comprehend the English they hear by requiring/requesting the speaker to repeat, slow down, or rephrase speech.

(C) Advanced. Advanced ELs have the ability to understand, with second language acquisition support, grade-appropriate spoken English used in academic and social settings. These students:

(i) usually understand longer, more elaborated directions, conversations, and discussions on familiar and some unfamiliar topics, but sometimes need processing time and sometimes depend on visuals, verbal cues, and gestures to support understanding;

(ii) understand most main points, most important details, and some implicit information during social and basic instructional interactions that have not been intentionally modified for ELs; and

(iii) occasionally require/request the speaker to repeat, slow down, or rephrase to clarify the meaning of the English they hear.

(D) Advanced high. Advanced high ELs have the ability to understand, with minimal second language acquisition support, grade-appropriate spoken English used in academic and social settings. These students:

(i) understand longer, elaborated directions, conversations, and discussions on familiar and unfamiliar topics with occasional need for processing time and with little dependence on visuals, verbal cues, and gestures; some exceptions when complex academic or highly specialized language is used;

(ii) understand main points, important details, and implicit information at a level nearly comparable to native English-speaking peers during social and instructional interactions; and

(iii) rarely require/request the speaker to repeat, slow down, or rephrase to clarify the meaning of the English they hear.

(2) Speaking, Kindergarten–Grade 12. ELs may be at the beginning, intermediate, advanced, or advanced high stage of English language acquisition in speaking. The following proficiency level descriptors for speaking are sufficient to describe the overall English language proficiency levels of ELs in this language domain in order to linguistically accommodate their instruction.

(A) Beginning. Beginning ELs have little or no ability to speak English in academic and social settings. These students:

(i) mainly speak using single words and short phrases consisting of recently practiced, memorized, or highly familiar material to get immediate needs met; may be hesitant to speak and often give up in their attempts to communicate;

(ii) speak using a very limited bank of high-frequency, high-need, concrete vocabulary, including key words and expressions needed for basic communication in academic and social contexts;

(iii) lack the knowledge of English grammar necessary to connect ideas and speak in sentences; can sometimes produce sentences using recently practiced, memorized, or highly familiar material;

(iv) exhibit second language acquisition errors that may hinder overall communication, particularly when trying to convey information beyond memorized, practiced, or highly familiar material; and

(v) typically use pronunciation that significantly inhibits communication.

(B) Intermediate. Intermediate ELs have the ability to speak in a simple manner using English commonly heard in routine academic and social settings. These students:

(i) are able to express simple, original messages, speak using sentences, and participate in short conversations and classroom interactions; may hesitate frequently and for long periods to think about how to communicate desired meaning;

(ii) speak simply using basic vocabulary needed in

everyday social interactions and routine academic contexts; rarely have vocabulary to speak in detail;

(iii) exhibit an emerging awareness of English grammar and speak using mostly simple sentence structures and simple tenses; are most comfortable speaking in present tense;

(iv) exhibit second language acquisition errors that may hinder overall communication when trying to use complex or less familiar English; and

(v) use pronunciation that can usually be understood by people accustomed to interacting with ELs.

(C) Advanced. Advanced ELs have the ability to speak using grade-appropriate English, with second language acquisition support, in academic and social settings. These students:

(i) are able to participate comfortably in most conversations and academic discussions on familiar topics, with some pauses to restate, repeat, or search for words and phrases to clarify meaning;

(ii) discuss familiar academic topics using content-based terms and common abstract vocabulary; can usually speak in some detail on familiar topics;

(iii) have a grasp of basic grammar features, including a basic ability to narrate and describe in present, past, and future tenses; have an emerging ability to use complex sentences and complex grammar features;

(iv) make errors that interfere somewhat with communication when using complex grammar structures, long sentences, and less familiar words and expressions; and

(v) may mispronounce words, but use pronunciation that can usually be understood by people not accustomed to interacting with ELs.

(D) Advanced high. Advanced high ELs have the ability to speak using grade-appropriate English, with minimal second language acquisition support, in academic and social settings. These students:

(i) are able to participate in extended discussions on a variety of social and grade-appropriate academic topics with only occasional disruptions, hesitations, or pauses;

(ii) communicate effectively using abstract and content-based vocabulary during classroom instructional tasks, with some exceptions when low-frequency or academically demanding vocabulary is needed; use many of the same idioms and colloquialisms as their native English-speaking peers;

(iii) can use English grammar structures and complex sentences to narrate and describe at a level nearly comparable to native English-speaking peers;

(iv) make few second language acquisition errors that interfere with overall communication; and

(v) may mispronounce words, but rarely use pronunciation that interferes with overall communication.

(3) Reading, Kindergarten–Grade 1. ELs in Kindergarten and Grade 1 may be at the beginning, intermediate, advanced, or advanced high stage of English language acquisition in reading. The following proficiency level descriptors for reading are sufficient to describe the overall English language proficiency levels of ELLs in this language domain in order to linguistically accommodate their instruction and should take into account developmental stages of emergent readers.

(A) Beginning. Beginning ELs have little or no ability to use the English language to build foundational reading skills. These students:

(i) derive little or no meaning from grade-appropriate stories read aloud in English, unless the stories are:

(I) read in short "chunks";

(II) controlled to include the little English they know such as language that is high frequency, concrete, and recently practiced; and

(III) accompanied by ample visual supports such

as illustrations, gestures, pantomime, and objects and by linguistic supports such as careful enunciation and slower speech;

(ii) begin to recognize and understand environmental print in English such as signs, labeled items, names of peers, and logos; and

(iii) have difficulty decoding most grade-appropriate English text because they:

(I) understand the meaning of very few words in English; and

(II) struggle significantly with sounds in spoken English words and with sound–symbol relationships due to differences between their primary language and English.

(B) Intermediate. Intermediate ELs have a limited ability to use the English language to build foundational reading skills. These students:

(i) demonstrate limited comprehension (key words and general meaning) of grade-appropriate stories read aloud in English, unless the stories include:

(I) predictable story lines;

(II) highly familiar topics;

(III) primarily high-frequency, concrete vocabulary;

(IV) short, simple sentences; and

(V) visual and linguistic supports;

(ii) regularly recognize and understand common environmental print in English such as signs, labeled items, names of peers, logos; and

(iii) have difficulty decoding grade-appropriate English text because they:

(I) understand the meaning of only those English words they hear frequently; and

(II) struggle with some sounds in English words and some sound–symbol relationships due to differences between their primary language and English.

(C) Advanced. Advanced ELs have the ability to use the English language, with second language acquisition support, to build foundational reading skills. These students:

(i) demonstrate comprehension of most main points and most supporting ideas in grade-appropriate stories read aloud in English, although they may still depend on visual and linguistic supports to gain or confirm meaning;

(ii) recognize some basic English vocabulary and high-frequency words in isolated print; and

(iii) with second language acquisition support, are able to decode most grade-appropriate English text because they:

(I) understand the meaning of most grade-appropriate English words; and

(II) have little difficulty with English sounds and sound–symbol relationships that result from differences between their primary language and English.

(D) Advanced high. Advanced high ELs have the ability to use the English language, with minimal second language acquisition support, to build foundational reading skills. These students:

(i) demonstrate, with minimal second language acquisition support and at a level nearly comparable to native English-speaking peers, comprehension of main points and supporting ideas (explicit and implicit) in grade-appropriate stories read aloud in English;

(ii) with some exceptions, recognize sight vocabulary and high-frequency words to a degree nearly comparable to that of native English-speaking peers; and

(iii) with minimal second language acquisition support, have an ability to decode and understand grade-appropriate English text at a level nearly comparable to native English-speaking peers.

(4) Reading, Grades 2–12. ELs in Grades 2–12 may be at the beginning, intermediate, advanced, or advanced high stage of English language acquisition in

reading. The following proficiency level descriptors for reading are sufficient to describe the overall English language proficiency levels of ELs in this language domain in order to linguistically accommodate their instruction.

(A) Beginning. Beginning ELs have little or no ability to read and understand English used in academic and social contexts. These students:

(i) read and understand the very limited recently practiced, memorized, or highly familiar English they have learned; vocabulary predominantly includes:

(I) environmental print;

(II) some very high-frequency words; and

(III) concrete words that can be represented by pictures;

(ii) read slowly, word by word;

(iii) have a very limited sense of English language structures;

(iv) comprehend predominantly isolated familiar words and phrases; comprehend some sentences in highly routine contexts or recently practiced, highly familiar text;

(v) are highly dependent on visuals and prior knowledge to derive meaning from text in English; and

(vi) are able to apply reading comprehension skills in English only when reading texts written for this level.

(B) Intermediate. Intermediate ELLs have the ability to read and understand simple, high-frequency English used in routine academic and social contexts. These students:

(i) read and understand English vocabulary on a somewhat wider range of topics and with increased depth; vocabulary predominantly includes:

(I) everyday oral language;

(II) literal meanings of common words;

(III) routine academic language and terms; and

(IV) commonly used abstract language such as terms used to describe basic feelings;

(ii) often read slowly and in short phrases; may re-read to clarify meaning;

(iii) have a growing understanding of basic, routinely used English language structures;

(iv) understand simple sentences in short, connected texts, but are dependent on visual cues, topic familiarity, prior knowledge, pretaught topic-related vocabulary, story predictability, and teacher/peer assistance to sustain comprehension;

(v) struggle to independently read and understand grade-level texts; and

(vi) are able to apply basic and some higher-order comprehension skills when reading texts that are linguistically accommodated and/or simplified for this level.

(C) Advanced. Advanced ELs have the ability to read and understand, with second language acquisition support, grade-appropriate English used in academic and social contexts. These students:

(i) read and understand, with second language acquisition support, a variety of grade-appropriate English vocabulary used in social and academic contexts:

(I) with second language acquisition support, read and understand grade-appropriate concrete and abstract vocabulary, but have difficulty with less commonly encountered words;

(II) demonstrate an emerging ability to understand words and phrases beyond their literal meaning; and

(III) understand multiple meanings of commonly used words;

(ii) read longer phrases and simple sentences from familiar text with appropriate rate and speed;

(iii) are developing skill in using their growing familiarity with English language structures to construct meaning of grade-appropriate text; and

(iv) are able to apply basic and higher-order comprehension skills when reading grade-appropriate text, but are still occasionally dependent on visuals, teacher/peer assistance, and other linguistically accommodated text features to determine or clarify meaning, particularly with unfamiliar topics.

(D) Advanced high. Advanced high ELs have the ability to read and understand, with minimal second language acquisition support, grade-appropriate English used in academic and social contexts. These students:

(i) read and understand vocabulary at a level nearly comparable to that of their native English-speaking peers, with some exceptions when low-frequency or specialized vocabulary is used;

(ii) generally read grade-appropriate, familiar text with appropriate rate, speed, intonation, and expression;

(iii) are able to, at a level nearly comparable to native English-speaking peers, use their familiarity with English language structures to construct meaning of grade-appropriate text; and

(iv) are able to apply, with minimal second language acquisition support and at a level nearly comparable to native English-speaking peers, basic and higher-order comprehension skills when reading grade-appropriate text.

(5) Writing, Kindergarten–Grade 1. ELs in Kindergarten and Grade 1 may be at the beginning, intermediate, advanced, or advanced high stage of English language acquisition in writing. The following proficiency level descriptors for writing are sufficient to describe the overall English language proficiency levels of ELLs in this language domain in order to linguistically accommodate their instruction and should take into account developmental stages of emergent writers.

(A) Beginning. Beginning ELs have little or no ability to use the English language to build foundational writing skills. These students:

(i) are unable to use English to explain self-generated writing such as stories they have created or other personal expressions, including emergent forms of writing (pictures, letter-like forms, mock words, scribbling, etc.);

(ii) know too little English to participate meaningfully in grade-appropriate shared writing activities using the English language;

(iii) cannot express themselves meaningfully in self-generated, connected written text in English beyond the level of high-frequency, concrete words, phrases, or short sentences that have been recently practiced and/or memorized; and

(iv) may demonstrate little or no awareness of English print conventions.

(B) Intermediate. Intermediate ELLs have a limited ability to use the English language to build foundational writing skills. These students:

(i) know enough English to explain briefly and simply self-generated writing, including emergent forms of writing, as long as the topic is highly familiar and concrete and requires very high-frequency English;

(ii) can participate meaningfully in grade-appropriate shared writing activities using the English language only when the writing topic is highly familiar and concrete and requires very high-frequency English;

(iii) express themselves meaningfully in self-generated, connected written text in English when their writing is limited to short sentences featuring simple, concrete English used frequently in class; and

(iv) frequently exhibit features of their primary language when writing in English such as primary language words, spelling patterns, word order, and literal translating.

(C) Advanced. Advanced ELs have the ability to use the English language to build, with second language acquisition support, foundational writing skills. These students:

(i) use predominantly grade-appropriate English to explain, in some detail, most self-generated writing, including emergent forms of writing;

(ii) can participate meaningfully, with second language acquisition support, in most grade-appropriate shared writing activities using the English language;

(iii) although second language acquisition support is needed, have an emerging ability to express themselves in self-generated, connected written text in English in a grade-appropriate manner; and

(iv) occasionally exhibit second language acquisition errors when writing in English.

(D) Advanced high. Advanced high ELLs have the ability to use the English language to build, with minimal second language acquisition support, foundational writing skills. These students:

(i) use English at a level of complexity and detail nearly comparable to that of native English-speaking peers when explaining self-generated writing, including emergent forms of writing;

(ii) can participate meaningfully in most grade-appropriate shared writing activities using the English language; and

(iii) although minimal second language acquisition

support may be needed, express themselves in self-generated, connected written text in English in a manner nearly comparable to their native English-speaking peers.

(6) Writing, Grades 2–12. ELLs in Grades 2–12 may be at the beginning, intermediate, advanced, or advanced high stage of English language acquisition in writing. The following proficiency level descriptors for writing are sufficient to describe the overall English language proficiency levels of ELs in this language domain in order to linguistically accommodate their instruction.

(A) Beginning. Beginning ELLs lack the English vocabulary and grasp of English language structures necessary to address grade-appropriate writing tasks meaningfully. These students:

(i) have little or no ability to use the English language to express ideas in writing and engage meaningfully in grade-appropriate writing assignments in content area instruction;

(ii) lack the English necessary to develop or demonstrate elements of grade-appropriate writing such as focus and coherence, conventions, organization, voice, and development of ideas in English; and

(iii) exhibit writing features typical at this level, including:

(I) ability to label, list, and copy;

(II) high-frequency words/phrases and short, simple sentences (or even short paragraphs) based primarily on recently practiced, memorized, or highly familiar material; this type of writing may be quite accurate;

(III) present tense used primarily; and

(IV) frequent primary language features (spelling patterns, word order, literal translations, and words from the student's primary language) and other errors associated with second language acquisition may significantly hinder or prevent understanding, even for individuals accustomed to the writing of ELs.

(B) Intermediate. Intermediate ELs have enough English vocabulary and enough grasp of English language structures to address grade-appropriate writing tasks in a limited way. These students:

(i) have a limited ability to use the English language to express ideas in writing and engage meaningfully in grade-appropriate writing assignments in content area instruction;

(ii) are limited in their ability to develop or demonstrate elements of grade-appropriate writing in English; communicate best when topics are highly familiar and concrete, and require simple, high-frequency English; and

(iii) exhibit writing features typical at this level, including:

(I) simple, original messages consisting of short, simple sentences; frequent inaccuracies occur when creating or taking risks beyond familiar English;

(II) high-frequency vocabulary; academic writing often has an oral tone;

(III) loosely connected text with limited use of cohesive devices or repetitive use, which may cause gaps in meaning;

(IV) repetition of ideas due to lack of vocabulary and language structures;

(V) present tense used most accurately; simple future and past tenses, if attempted, are used inconsistently or with frequent inaccuracies;

(VI) undetailed descriptions, explanations, and narrations; difficulty expressing abstract ideas;

(VII) primary language features and errors associated with second language acquisition may be frequent; and

(VIII) some writing may be understood only by individuals accustomed to the writing of ELs; parts of the writing may be hard to understand even for individuals accustomed to ELL writing.

(C) Advanced. Advanced ELs have enough English vocabulary and command of English language structures to address grade-appropriate writing tasks, although second language acquisition support is needed. These students:

(i) are able to use the English language, with second language acquisition support, to express ideas in writing and engage meaningfully in grade-appropriate writing assignments in content area instruction;

(ii) know enough English to be able to develop or demonstrate elements of grade-appropriate writing in English, although second language acquisition support is particularly needed when topics are abstract, academically challenging, or unfamiliar; and

(iii) exhibit writing features typical at this level, including:

(I) grasp of basic verbs, tenses, grammar features, and sentence patterns; partial grasp of more complex verbs, tenses, grammar features, and sentence patterns;

(II) emerging grade-appropriate vocabulary; academic writing has a more academic tone;

(III) use of a variety of common cohesive devices, although some redundancy may occur;

(IV) narrations, explanations, and descriptions developed in some detail with emerging clarity; quality or quantity declines when abstract ideas are expressed, academic demands are high, or low-frequency vocabulary is required;

(V) occasional second language acquisition errors; and

(VI) communications are usually understood by individuals not accustomed to the writing of ELs.

(D) Advanced high. Advanced high ELs have acquired the English vocabulary and command of English language structures necessary to address grade-appropriate writing tasks with minimal second language acquisition support. These students:

(i) are able to use the English language, with minimal second language acquisition support, to express ideas in writing and engage meaningfully in grade-appropriate writing assignments in content area instruction;

(ii) know enough English to be able to develop or demonstrate, with minimal second language acquisition support, elements of grade-appropriate writing in English; and

(iii) exhibit writing features typical at this level, including:

(I) nearly comparable to writing of native English-speaking peers in clarity and precision with regard to English vocabulary and language structures, with occasional exceptions when writing about academically complex ideas, abstract ideas, or topics requiring low-frequency vocabulary;

(II) occasional difficulty with naturalness of phrasing and expression; and

(III) errors associated with second language acquisition are minor and usually limited to low-frequency words and structures; errors rarely interfere with communication.

(E) Effective date. The provisions of this section supersede the ESL standards specified in Chapter 128 of this title (relating to Texas Essential Knowledge and Skills for Spanish Language Arts and English as a Second Language) upon the effective date of this section.

Source: The provisions of this §74.4 adopted to be effective December 25, 2007, 32 TexReg 9615.

Chapter 89

Adaptations for Special Populations Subchapter BB.
Commissioner's Rules Concerning State Plan for Educating
Limited English Proficient Students

§89.1201. Policy.

(a) It is the policy of the state that every student in the state who has a primary language other than English and who is identified as an English learner shall be provided a full opportunity to participate in a bilingual education or English as a second language (ESL) program, as required in the Texas Education Code (TEC), Chapter 29, Subchapter B. To ensure equal educational opportunity, as required in the TEC, §1.002(a), each school district shall:

(1) identify English learners based on criteria established by the state;

(2) provide bilingual education and ESL programs, as integral parts of the general program as described in the TEC, §4.002;

(3) seek appropriately certified teaching personnel to ensure that English learners are afforded full opportunity to master the essential knowledge and skills required by the state; and

(4) assess achievement for essential knowledge and skills in accordance with the TEC, Chapter 29, to ensure accountability for English learners and the schools that serve them.

(b) The goal of bilingual education programs shall be to enable English learners to become competent in listening, speaking, reading, and writing in the English language through the development of literacy and academic skills in the primary language and English. Such programs shall emphasize the mastery of English language skills, as well as mathematics, science, and social studies, as integral parts of the academic goals for all students to enable English learners to participate equitably in school.

(c) The goal of ESL programs shall be to enable English learners to become competent in listening, speaking, reading, and writing in the English language through the integrated use of second language acquisition methods. The ESL program shall emphasize the mastery of English language skills, as well as mathematics, science, and social studies, as integral parts of the academic goals for all students to enable English learners to participate equitably in school.

(d) Bilingual education and ESL programs shall be integral parts of the total school program. Such programs shall use instructional approaches designed to meet the specific language needs of English learners. The basic curriculum content of the programs shall be based on the Texas Essential Knowledge and Skills and the English language proficiency standards required by the state.

Statutory Authority: The provisions of this §89.1201 issued under the Texas Education Code, §§29.051, 29.053, 29.054, 29.055, 29.056, 29.0561, 29.057, 29.058, 29.059, 29.060, 29.061, 29.062, 29.063, 29.064, and 29.066.

Source: The provisions of this §89.1201 adopted to be effective September 1, 1996, 21 TexReg 5700; amended to be effective May 28, 2012, 37 TexReg 3822; amended to be effective July 15, 2018, 43 TexReg 4731.

§89.1203. Definitions.

The following words and terms, when used in this subchapter, shall have the following meanings, unless the context clearly indicates otherwise.

(1) Bilingual education allotment--An adjusted basic funding allotment provided for each school district based on student average daily attendance in a bilingual education or special language program in accordance with Texas Education Code (TEC), §42.153.

(2) Certified English as a second language teacher--The term "certified English as a second language teacher" as used in this subchapter is synonymous with the term "professional transitional language educator" used in TEC, §29.063.

(3) Dual language immersion--A state-approved bilingual program model in accordance with TEC, §29.066.

(4) Dual-language instruction--An educational approach that focuses on the use of English and the student's primary language for instructional purposes.

(5) English as a second language program--A special language program in accordance with TEC, Chapter 29.

(6) English language proficiency standards (ELPS)--Standards to be published along with the Texas Essential Knowledge and Skills for each subject in the required curriculum outlined in Chapter 74 of this title (relating to Curriculum Requirements), including foundation and enrichment areas, ELPS, and college and career readiness standards.

(7) English learner--A student who is in the process of acquiring English and has another language as the primary language. The terms English language learner and English learner are used interchangeably and are synonymous with limited English proficient (LEP) student, as used in TEC, Chapter 29, Subchapter B.

(8) Exit--The point when a student is no longer classified as LEP (i.e., the student is reclassified), no longer requires bilingual or special language program services, and is classified as non-LEP in the Texas Student Data System Public Education Information Management System (TSDS PEIMS). The term "exit" as used in this subchapter is synonymous with the description in TEC, Chapter 29, of "transferring out" of bilingual or special language programming.

(9) Reclassification--The process by which the language proficiency assessment committee determines that an English learner has met the appropriate criteria to be classified as non-LEP and is coded as such in TSDS PEIMS.

(10) School district--For the purposes of this subchapter, the definition of a school district includes an open-enrollment charter school.

Statutory Authority: The provisions of this §89.1203 issued under the Texas Education Code, §§29.051, 29.053, 29.054, 29.055, 29.056, 29.0561, 29.057, 29.058, 29.059, 29.060, 29.061, 29.062, 29.063, 29.064, and 29.066.

Source: The provisions of this §89.1203 adopted to be effective May 28, 2012, 37 TexReg 3822; amended to be effective July 15, 2018, 43 TexReg 4731.

§89.1205. Required Bilingual Education and English as a Second Language Programs.

(a) Each school district that has an enrollment of 20 or more English learners in any language classification in the same grade level district-wide shall offer a bilingual education program as described in subsection (b) of this section for the English learners in prekindergarten through the elementary grades who speak that language. "Elementary grades" shall include at least prekindergarten through Grade 5; sixth grade shall be included when clustered with elementary grades.

(b) A school district shall provide a bilingual education program by offering dual-language instruction (English and primary language) in prekindergarten through the elementary grades, using one of the four bilingual program models described in §89.1210 of this title (relating to Program Content and Design).

(c) All English learners for whom a school district is not required to offer a bilingual education program shall be provided an English as a second language (ESL) program as described in subsection (d) of this section, regardless of the students' grade levels and primary language, and regardless of the number of such students, except in cases where a district exercises the option described in subsection (g) of this section.

(d) A school district shall provide ESL instruction by offering an ESL program using one of the two models described in §89.1210 of this title.

(e) School districts may join with other school districts to provide bilingual education or ESL programs.

(f) In addition to the required bilingual and/or ESL programs, school districts are authorized to establish a bilingual education program even if they have an enrollment of fewer than 20 English learners in any language classification in the same grade level district-wide and are not required to do so under subsection (a) of this section. Under this authorization, school districts shall adhere to all program requirements as described in §§89.1210, 89.1227, 89.1228, and 89.1229 of this title.

(g) In addition to the required bilingual and/or ESL programs, school districts are authorized to establish a bilingual education program at grade levels in which the bilingual education program is not required under subsection (a) of this section. Under this authorization, school districts shall adhere to all program requirements as described in §§89.1210, 89.1227, 89.1228, and 89.1229 of this title.

Statutory Authority: The provisions of this §89.1205 issued under the Texas Education Code, §§29.051, 29.053, 29.054, 29.055, 29.056, 29.0561, 29.057, 29.058, 29.059, 29.060, 29.061, 29.062, 29.063, 29.064, and 29.066.

Source: The provisions of this §89.1205 adopted to be effective September 1, 1996, 21 TexReg 5700; amended to be effective March 5, 1999, 24 TexReg 1383; amended to be effective April 18, 2002, 27 TexReg 3107; amended to be effective September 17, 2007, 32 TexReg 6311; amended to be effective May 28, 2012, 37 TexReg 3822; amended to be effective July 15, 2018, 43 TexReg 4731.

§89.1207. Bilingual Education Exceptions and English as a Second Language Waivers.

(a) Bilingual education program.

(1) Exceptions. A school district that is unable to provide a bilingual education program as required by §89.1205(a) of this title (relating to Required Bilingual Education and English as a Second Language Programs) because of an insufficient number of appropriately certified teachers shall request from the commissioner of education an exception to the bilingual education program and the approval of an alternative program. The approval of an exception to the bilingual education program shall be valid only during the school year for which it was granted. A request for a bilingual education program exception must be submitted by November 1 and shall include:

(A) a statement of the reasons the school district is unable to provide a sufficient number of appropriately certified teachers to offer the bilingual education program with supporting documentation;

(B) a description of the alternative instructional program and methods to meet the affective, linguistic, and cognitive needs of the English learners, including the manner through which the students will be given opportunity to master the essential knowledge and skills required by Chapter 74 of this title (relating to Curriculum Requirements) to include foundation and enrichment areas, English language proficiency standards (ELPS), and college and career readiness standards (CCRS);

(C) an assurance that appropriately certified teachers available in the school district will be assigned to grade levels beginning at prekindergarten followed successively by subsequent grade levels to ensure that the linguistic and academic needs of the English learners with beginning levels of English proficiency are served on a priority basis;

(D) an assurance that the school district will implement a comprehensive professional development plan that:

(i) is ongoing and targets the development of the knowledge, skills, and competencies needed to serve the needs of English learners;

(ii) includes the teachers who are not certified or not appropriately certified who are assigned to implement the proposed alternative program; and

(iii) may include additional teachers who work with English learners;

(E) an assurance that at least 10% of the bilingual education allotment shall be used to fund the comprehensive professional development plan required under subparagraph (D) of this paragraph;

(F) an assurance that the school district will take actions to ensure that the program required under §89.1205(a) of this title will be provided the subsequent year, including its plans for recruiting an adequate number of appropriately certified teachers to eliminate the need for subsequent exceptions and measurable targets for the subsequent year; and

(G) an assurance that the school district shall satisfy the additional reporting requirements described in §89.1265(c) of this title (relating to Evaluation).

(2) Documentation. A school district submitting a bilingual education exception shall maintain written records of all documents supporting the submission and assurances listed in paragraph (1) of this subsection, including:

(A) a description of the proposed alternative instructional program designed to meet the affective, linguistic, and cognitive needs of the English learners;

(B) the number of teachers for whom a bilingual education exception is needed by grade level and per campus;

(C) a copy of the school district's comprehensive professional development plan; and

(D) a copy of the bilingual allotment budget documenting that a minimum of 10% of the funds were used to fund the comprehensive professional development plan.

(3) Approval of exceptions. Bilingual education program exceptions will be granted by the commissioner if the requesting school district:

(A) meets or exceeds the state average for English learner performance on the required state assessments;

(B) meets the requirements and measurable targets of the action plan described in paragraph (1)(F) of this subsection submitted the previous year and approved by the Texas Education Agency (TEA); or

(C) reduces by 25% the number of teachers under exception for bilingual programs when compared to the number of exceptions granted the previous year.

(4) Denial of exceptions. A school district denied a bilingual education program exception must submit to the commissioner a detailed action plan for complying with required regulations for the following school year.

(5) Appeals. A school district denied a bilingual education program exception may appeal to the commissioner or the commissioner's designee. The decision of the commissioner or commissioner's designee is final and may not be appealed further.

(6) Special accreditation investigation. The commissioner may authorize a special accreditation investigation under the Texas Education Code (TEC), §39.057, if a school district is denied a bilingual education program exception for more than three consecutive years.

(7) Sanctions. Based on the results of a special accreditation investigation, the commissioner may take appropriate action under the TEC, §39.102.

(b) English as a second language (ESL) program.

(1) Waivers. A school district that is unable to provide an ESL program as required by §89.1205(c) of this title because of an insufficient number of appropriately certified teachers shall request from the commissioner a waiver of the certification requirements for each teacher who will provide instruction in ESL for English learners. The approval of a waiver of certification requirements shall be valid only during the school year for which it was granted. A request for an ESL program waiver must be submitted by November 1 and shall include:

(A) a statement of the reasons the school district is unable to provide a sufficient number of appropriately certified teachers to offer the ESL program;

(B) a description of the alternative instructional program, including the manner in which the teachers in the ESL program will meet the affective, linguistic, and cognitive needs of the English learners, including the manner through which the students will be given opportunity to master the essential knowledge and skills required by Chapter 74 of this title to include foundation and enrichment areas, ELPS, and CCRS;

(C) an assurance that appropriately certified teachers available in the school district will be assigned to grade levels beginning at prekindergarten followed successively by subsequent grade levels in the elementary school campus and, if needed, secondary campuses, to ensure that the linguistic and academic needs of the English learners with the lower levels of English proficiency are served on a priority basis;

(D) an assurance that the school district shall implement a comprehensive professional development plan that:

(i) is ongoing and targets the development of the knowledge, skills, and competencies needed to serve the needs of English learners;

(ii) includes the teachers who are not certified or not appropriately certified who are assigned to implement the proposed alternative program;

and

(iii) may include additional teachers who work with English learners;

(E) an assurance that at least 10% of the bilingual education allotment shall be used to fund the comprehensive professional development plan required under subparagraph (D) of this paragraph;

(F) an assurance that the school district will take actions to ensure that the program required under §89.1205(c) of this title will be provided the subsequent year, including its plans for recruiting an adequate number of appropriately certified teachers to eliminate the need for subsequent waivers; and

(G) an assurance that the school district shall satisfy the additional reporting requirements described in §89.1265(c) of this title.

(2) Documentation. A school district submitting an ESL waiver shall maintain written records of all documents supporting the submission and assurances listed in paragraph (1) of this subsection, including:

(A) a description of the proposed alternative instructional program designed to meet the affective, linguistic, and cognitive needs of the English learners;

(B) the name and teaching assignment, per campus, of each teacher who is assigned to implement the ESL program and is under a waiver and the estimated date for the completion of the ESL supplemental certification, which must be completed by the end of the school year for which the waiver was requested;

(C) a copy of the school district's comprehensive professional development plan;

(D) a copy of the bilingual allotment budget documenting that a minimum of 10% of the funds were used to fund the comprehensive professional development plan; and

(E) a description of the actions taken to recruit an adequate number of appropriately certified teachers.

(3) Approval of waivers. ESL waivers will be granted by the commissioner if the requesting school district:

(A) meets or exceeds the state average for English learner performance on the required state assessments; or

(B) meets the requirements and measurable targets of the action plan described in paragraph (1)(G) of this subsection submitted the previous year and approved by the TEA.

(4) Denial of waivers. A school district denied an ESL program waiver must submit to the commissioner a detailed action plan for complying with required regulations for the following school year.

(5) Appeals. A school district denied an ESL waiver may appeal to the commissioner or the commissioner's designee. The decision of the commissioner or commissioner's designee is final and may not be appealed further.

(6) Special accreditation investigation. The commissioner may authorize a special accreditation investigation under the TEC, §39.057, if a school district is denied an ESL waiver for more than three consecutive years.

(7) Sanctions. Based on the results of a special accreditation investigation, the commissioner may take appropriate action under the TEC, §39.102.

Statutory Authority: The provisions of this §89.1207 issued under the Texas Education Code, §§29.051, 29.053, 29.054, 29.055, 29.056, 29.0561, 29.057, 29.058, 29.059, 29.060, 29.061, 29.062, 29.063, 29.064, and 29.066.

Source: The provisions of this §89.1207 adopted to be effective September 17, 2007, 32 TexReg 6311; amended to be effective May 28, 2012, 37 TexReg 3822; amended to be effective July 15, 2018, 43 TexReg 4731.

§89.1210. Program Content and Design.

(a) Each school district required to offer a bilingual education or English as a second language (ESL) program shall provide each English learner the opportunity to be enrolled in the required program at his or her grade level. Each student's level of proficiency shall be designated by the language proficiency assessment committee in accordance with §89.1220(g) of this title (relating to Language Proficiency Assessment Committee). The school district shall accommodate the instruction, pacing, and materials to ensure that English learners have a full opportunity to master the essential knowledge and skills of the required curriculum, which includes the Texas Essential Knowledge and Skills and English language proficiency standards (ELPS). Students participating in the bilingual education program may demonstrate their mastery of the essential knowledge and skills in either their primary language or in English for each content area.

(1) A bilingual education program of instruction established by a school district shall be a full-time program of dual-language instruction (English and primary language) that provides for learning basic skills in the primary language of the students enrolled in the program and for carefully structured and sequenced mastery of English language skills under Texas Education Code (TEC), §29.055(a).

(2) An ESL program of instruction established by a school district shall be a program of intensive instruction in English in which ESL teachers recognize and address language differences in accordance with TEC, §29.055(a).

(b) The bilingual education program and ESL program shall be integral parts of the general educational program required under Chapter 74 of this title (relating to Curriculum Requirements) to include foundation and enrichment areas, ELPS, and college and career readiness standards. In bilingual education programs, school districts shall purchase instructional materials in both program languages with the district's instructional materials allotment or otherwise acquire instructional materials for use in bilingual education classes in accordance with TEC, §31.029(a). Instructional materials for bilingual education programs on the list adopted by the commissioner of education, as provided by TEC, §31.0231, may be used as curriculum tools to enhance the learning process. The school district shall provide for ongoing coordination between the bilingual/ESL program and the general educational program. The bilingual education and ESL programs shall address the affective, linguistic, and cognitive needs of English learners as follows.

(1) Affective.

(A) English learners in a bilingual program shall be provided instruction using second language acquisition methods in their primary language to introduce basic concepts of the school environment, and content instruction both in their primary language and in English, which instills confidence, self-assurance, and a positive identity with their cultural heritages. The program shall be designed to consider the students' learning experiences and shall incorporate the cultural aspects of the students' backgrounds in accordance with TEC, §29.055(b).

(B) English learners in an ESL program shall be provided instruction using second language acquisition methods in English to introduce basic concepts of the school environment, which instills confidence, self-assurance, and a positive identity with their cultural heritages. The program shall be designed to incorporate the students' primary languages and learning experiences and shall incorporate the cultural aspects of the students' backgrounds in accordance with TEC, §29.055(b).

(2) Linguistic.

(A) English learners in a bilingual program shall be provided intensive instruction in the skills of listening, speaking, reading, and writing both in their primary language and in English, provided through the ELPS. The instruction in both languages shall be structured to ensure that the students master the required essential knowledge and skills and higher-order thinking skills in all subjects.

(B) English learners in an ESL program shall be provided intensive instruction to develop proficiency in listening, speaking, reading, and writing in the English language, provided through the ELPS. The instruction in academic content areas shall be structured to ensure that the students master the required essential knowledge and skills and higher-order thinking skills in all subjects.

(3) Cognitive.

(A) English learners in a bilingual program shall be provided instruction in language arts, mathematics, science, and social studies both in their primary language and in English, using second language acquisition methods in either their primary language, in English, or in both, depending on the specific program model(s) implemented by the district. The content area instruction in both languages shall be structured to ensure that the students master the required essential knowledge and skills and higher-order thinking skills in all subjects.

(B) English learners in an ESL program shall be provided instruction in English in language arts, mathematics, science, and social studies using second language acquisition methods. The instruction in academic content areas shall be structured to ensure that the students master the required essential knowledge and skills and higher-order thinking skills.

(c) The bilingual education program shall be implemented through at least one of the following program models.

(1) Transitional bilingual/early exit is a bilingual program model in which students identified as Eng-lish learners are served in both English and another language and are prepared to meet reclassification criteria to be successful in English-only instruction not earlier than two or later than five years after the student enrolls in school. Instruction in this program is delivered by a teacher appropriately certified in bilingual education under TEC, §29.061(b)(1), for the assigned grade level and content area. The goal of early-exit transitional bilingual education is for program participants to use their primary language as a resource while acquiring full proficiency in English. This model provides instruction in literacy and academic content through the medium of the students' primary language along with instruction in English that targets second language development through academic content.

(2) Transitional bilingual/late exit is a bilingual program model in which students identified as English learners are served in both English and another language and are prepared to meet reclassification criteria to be successful in English-only instruction not earlier than six or later than seven years after the student enrolls in school. Instruction in this program is delivered by a teacher appropriately certified in bilingual education under TEC, §29.061(b)(2), for the assigned grade level and content area. The goal of late-exit transitional bilingual education is for program participants to use their primary language as a resource while acquiring full proficiency in English. This model provides instruction in literacy and academic content through the medium of the students' primary language along with instruction in English that targets second language development through academic content.

(3) Dual language immersion/one-way is a bilingual/biliteracy program model in which students identified as English learners are served in both English and another language and are prepared to meet reclassification criteria in order to be successful in English-only instruction not earlier than six or later than seven years after the student enrolls in school. Instruction provided in a language other than English in this program model is delivered by a teacher appropriately certified in bilingual educa-

tion under TEC, §29.061. Instruction provided in English in this program model may be delivered either by a teacher appropriately certified in bilingual education or by a different teacher certified in ESL in accordance with TEC, §29.061. The goal of one-way dual language immersion is for program participants to attain full proficiency in another language as well as English. This model provides ongoing instruction in literacy and academic content in the students' primary language as well as English, with at least half of the instruction delivered in the students' primary language for the duration of the program.

(4) Dual language immersion/two-way is a bilingual/biliteracy program model in which students identified as English learners are integrated with students proficient in English and are served in both English and another language and are prepared to meet reclassification criteria in order to be successful in English-only instruction not earlier than six or later than seven years after the student enrolls in school. Instruction provided in a language other than English in this program model is delivered by a teacher appropriately certified in bilingual education under TEC, §29.061, for the assigned grade level and content area. Instruction provided in English in this program model may be delivered either by a teacher appropriately certified in bilingual education or by a different teacher certified in ESL in accordance with TEC, §29.061, for the assigned grade level and content area. The goal of two-way dual language immersion is for program participants to attain full proficiency in another language as well as English. This model provides ongoing instruction in literacy and academic content in English and another language with at least half of the instruction delivered in the non-English program language for the duration of the program.

(d) The ESL program shall be implemented through one of the following program models.

(1) An ESL/content-based program model is an English acquisition program that serves students identified as English learners through English instruction by a teacher appropriately certified in ESL under TEC, §29.061(c), through English language arts and reading, mathematics, science, and social studies. The goal of content-based ESL is for English learners to attain full proficiency in English in order to participate equitably in school. This model targets English language development through academic content instruction that is linguistically and culturally responsive in English language arts and reading, mathematics, science, and social studies.

(2) An ESL/pull-out program model is an English acquisition program that serves students identified as English learners through English instruction provided by an appropriately certified ESL teacher under the TEC, §29.061(c), through English language arts and reading. The goal of ESL pull-out is for English learners to attain full proficiency in English in order to participate equitably in school. This model targets English language development through academic content instruction that is linguistically and culturally responsive in English language arts and reading. Instruction shall be provided by the ESL teacher in a pull-out or inclusionary delivery model.

(e) Except in the courses specified in subsection (f) of this section, second language acquisition methods, which may involve the use of the students' primary language, may be provided in any of the courses or electives required for promotion or graduation to assist the English learners to master the essential knowledge and skills for the required subject(s). The use of second language acquisition methods shall not impede the awarding of credit toward meeting promotion or graduation requirements.

(f) In subjects such as art, music, and physical education, English learners shall participate with their English-speaking peers in general education classes provided in the subjects. As noted in TEC, §29.055(d), elective courses included in the curriculum may be taught in a language other than English. The school district shall ensure that students enrolled in bilingual education and ESL programs have a meaningful opportunity to participate with other students in all extracurricular activities.

(g) The required bilingual education or ESL program shall be provided to every English learner with parental approval until such time that the student meets exit criteria as described in §89.1225(i) of this title (relating to Testing and Classification of Students) or §89.1226(i) of this title (relating to Testing and Classification of Students, Beginning with School Year 2019-2020) or graduates from high school.

Statutory Authority: The provisions of this §89.1210 issued under the Texas Education Code, §§29.051, 29.053, 29.054, 29.055, 29.056, 29.0561, 29.057, 29.058, 29.059, 29.060, 29.061, 29.062, 29.063, 29.064, and 29.066.

Source: The provisions of this §89.1210 adopted to be effective September 1, 1996, 21 TexReg 5700; amended to be effective March 5, 1999, 24 TexReg 1383; amended to be effective April 18, 2002, 27 TexReg 3107; amended to be effective May 28, 2012, 37 TexReg 3822; amended to be effective July 15, 2018, 43 TexReg 4731.

§89.1215. Home Language Survey.

(a) School districts shall administer only one home language survey to each new student enrolling for the first time in a Texas public school in any grade from prekindergarten through Grade 12. School districts shall require that the survey be signed by the student's parent or guardian for each student in prekindergarten through Grade 8 or by the student in Grades 9-12 as permitted under the Texas Education Code, §29.056(a)(1). The original copy of the survey shall be kept in the student's permanent record.

(b) The home language survey shall be administered in English, Spanish, and Vietnamese; for students of other language groups, the home language survey shall be translated into the primary language whenever possible. The home language survey shall contain the following questions.

(1) "What language is spoken in the child's home most of the time?"

(2) "What language does the child speak most of the time?"

(c) If the response on the home language survey indicates that a language other than English is used, the student shall be tested in accordance with §89.1225 of this title (relating to Testing and Classification of Students) or §89.1226 of this title (relating to Testing and Classification of Students, Beginning with School Year 2019-2020).

(d) For students previously enrolled in a Texas public school, the receiving district shall secure the student records, including the home language survey. All attempts to contact the sending district to request records shall be documented. Multiple attempts to obtain the student's home language survey shall be made. If attempts to obtain the student's home language survey from the sending district are unsuccessful, the identification process shall begin while attempts to contact the sending district for records continue throughout the four-week testing and identification period.

Statutory Authority: The provisions of this §89.1215 issued under the Texas Education Code, §§29.051, 29.053, 29.054, 29.055, 29.056, 29.0561, 29.057, 29.058, 29.059, 29.060, 29.061, 29.062, 29.063, 29.064, and 29.066.

Source: The provisions of this §89.1215 adopted to be effective September 1, 1996, 21 TexReg 5700; amended to be effective May 28, 2012, 37 TexReg 3822; amended to be effective July 15, 2018, 43 TexReg 4731.

§89.1220. Language Proficiency Assessment Committee.

(a) School districts shall by local board policy establish and operate a language proficiency assessment committee. The school district shall have on file policy and procedures for the selection, appointment, and training of members of the language proficiency assessment committee(s).

(b) The language proficiency assessment committee shall include an appropriately certified bilingual educator (for students served through a bilingual education program), an appropriately certified English as a second language (ESL) educator (for students served through an ESL program), a parent of an English learner participating in a bilingual or ESL program, and a campus administrator in accordance with Texas Education Code (TEC), §29.063.

(c) In addition to the three required members of the language proficiency assessment committee, the school district may add other trained members to the committee.

(d) No parent serving on the language proficiency assessment committee shall be an employee of the school district.

(e) A school district shall establish and operate a sufficient number of language proficiency assessment committees to enable them to discharge their duties within four weeks of the enrollment of English learners.

(f) All members of the language proficiency assessment committee, including parents, shall be acting for the school district and shall observe all laws and rules governing confidentiality of information concerning individual students. The school district shall be responsible for the orientation and training of all members, including the parents, of the language proficiency assessment committee.

(g) Upon their initial enrollment and at the end of each school year, the language proficiency assessment committee shall review all pertinent information on all English learners identified in accordance with §89.1225(f) of this title (relating to Testing and Classification of Students) or §89.1226 of this title

(relating to Testing and Classification of Students, Beginning with School Year 2019-2020) and shall:

(1) designate the language proficiency level of each English learner in accordance with the guidelines issued pursuant to §89.1225(b)-(f) or §89.1226(b)-(f) of this title;

(2) designate the level of academic achievement of each English learner;

(3) designate, subject to parental approval, the initial instructional placement of each English learner in the required program;

(4) facilitate the participation of English learners in other special programs for which they are eligible while ensuring full access to the language program services required under the TEC, §29.053; and

(5) reclassify students, at the end of the school year only, as English proficient in accordance with the criteria described in §89.1225(i) or §89.1226(i) of this title.

(h) The language proficiency assessment committee shall give written notice to the student's parent or guardian, advising that the student has been classified as an English learner and requesting approval to place the student in the required bilingual education or ESL program not later than the 10th calendar day after the date of the student's classification in accordance with TEC, §29.056. The notice shall include information about the benefits of the bilingual education or ESL program for which the student has been recommended and that it is an integral part of the school program.

(i) Before the administration of the state criterion-referenced test each year, the language proficiency assessment committee shall determine the appropriate assessment option for each English learner as outlined in Chapter 101, Subchapter AA, of this title (relating to Commissioner's Rules Concerning the Participation of English Language Learners in State Assessments).

(j) Pending parent approval of an English learner's entry into the bilingual education or ESL program recommended by the language proficiency assessment committee, the school district shall place the student in the recommended program. Only English learners with parent approval who are receiving services will be included in the bilingual education allotment.

(k) The language proficiency assessment committee shall monitor the academic progress of each student who has met criteria for exit in accordance with TEC, §29.056(g), for the first two years after reclassification. If the student earns a failing grade in a subject in the foundation curriculum under TEC, §28.002(a)(1), during any grading period in the first two school years after the student is reclassified, the language proficiency assessment committee shall determine, based on the student's second language acquisition needs, whether the student may require intensive instruction or should be reenrolled in a bilingual education or special language program. In accordance with TEC, §29.0561, the language proficiency assessment committee shall review the student's performance and consider:

(1) the total amount of time the student was enrolled in a bilingual education or special language program;

(2) the student's grades each grading period in each subject in the foundation curriculum under TEC, §28.002(a)(1);

(3) the student's performance on each assessment instrument administered under TEC, §39.023(a) or (c);

(4) the number of credits the student has earned toward high school graduation, if applicable; and

(5) any disciplinary actions taken against the student under TEC, Chapter 37, Subchapter A (Alternative Settings for Behavior Management).

(l) The student's permanent record shall contain documentation of all actions impacting the English learner.

(1) Documentation shall include:

(A) the identification of the student as an English learner;

(B) the designation of the student's level of language proficiency;

(C) the recommendation of program placement;

(D) parental approval of entry or placement into the program;

(E) the dates of entry into, and placement within, the program;

(F) assessment information as outlined in Chapter 101, Subchapter AA, of this title;

(G) additional instructional interventions provided to address the specific language needs of the student;

(H) the date of exit from the program and parental approval;

(I) the results of monitoring for academic success, including students formerly classified as English learners, as required under the TEC, §29.063(c)(4); and

(J) the home language survey.

(2) Current documentation as described in paragraph (1) of this subsection shall be forwarded in the same manner as other student records to another school district in which the student enrolls.

(m) A school district may identify, exit, or place a student in a program without written approval of the student's parent or guardian if:

(1) the student is 18 years of age or has had the disabilities of minority removed;

(2) the parent or legal guardian provides approval through a phone conversation or e-mail that is documented in writing and retained; or

(3) an adult who the school district recognizes as standing in parental relation to the student provides written approval. This may include a foster parent or employee of a state or local governmental agency with temporary possession or control of the student.

Statutory Authority: The provisions of this §89.1220 issued under the Texas Education Code, §§29.051, 29.053, 29.054, 29.055, 29.056, 29.0561, 29.057, 29.058, 29.059, 29.060, 29.061, 29.062, 29.063, 29.064, and 29.066.

Source: The provisions of this §89.1220 adopted to be effective September 1, 1996, 21 TexReg 5700; amended to be effective March 5, 1999, 24 TexReg 1383; amended to be effective April 18, 2002, 27 TexReg 3107; amended to be effective September 17, 2007, 32 TexReg 6311; amended to be effective May 28, 2012, 37 TexReg 3822; amended to be effective July 15, 2018, 43 TexReg 4731.

§89.1225. Testing and Classification of Students.

(a) Beginning with school year 2019-2020, the provisions of this section shall expire and be superseded by the provisions in §89.1226 of this title (relating to Testing and Classification of Students, Beginning with School Year 2019-2020).

(b) Within four weeks of initial enrollment in a Texas public school, a student with a language other than English indicated on the home language survey shall be administered the required oral language proficiency test in prekindergarten through Grade 12 and norm-referenced standardized achievement instrument in Grades 2-12 as described in subsection (c) of this section and shall be identified as an English learner and placed in the required bilingual education or English as a second language (ESL) program in accordance with the criteria listed in subsection (f) of this section.

(c) For identifying English learners, school districts shall administer to each student who has a language other than English as identified on the home language survey:

(1) in prekindergarten through Grade 1, an oral language proficiency test approved by the Texas Education Agency (TEA); and

(2) in Grades 2-12, a TEA-approved oral language proficiency test and the English reading and English language arts sections from a TEA-approved norm-referenced assessment.

(d) School districts that provide a bilingual education program at the elementary grades shall administer an oral language proficiency test in the primary language of the student who is eligible to be served in the bilingual education program. If the primary language of the student is Spanish, the school district shall administer a Spanish TEA-approved oral language proficiency test. If a TEA-approved language proficiency test is not available in the primary language of the student, the school district shall determine the student's level of proficiency using informal oral language assessment measures.

(e) All of the language proficiency testing shall be administered by professionals or paraprofessionals who are proficient in the language of the test and trained in the language proficiency testing requirements of the test publisher.

(f) For entry into a bilingual education or ESL program, a student shall be identified as an English learner using the following criteria.

(1) In prekindergarten through Grade 1, the student's score on the English oral language proficiency test is below the level designated for indicating English proficiency.

(2) In Grades 2-12:

(A) the student's score on the English oral language proficiency test is below the level designated for indicating English proficiency; and

(B) the student's score on the English reading and/or English language arts sections of the TEA-approved norm-referenced standardized achievement instrument at his or her grade level is below the 40th percentile.

(g) A student shall be identified as an English learner if the student's ability in English is so limited that the English oral language proficiency or norm-referenced assessments described in subsection (c) of this section cannot be administered.

(h) The language proficiency assessment committee in conjunction with the admission, review, and dismissal (ARD) committee shall identify a student as an English learner if the student's ability in English is so limited or the student's disabilities are so severe that the English oral language proficiency or norm-referenced assessments described in subsection (c) of this section cannot be administered. The decision for entry into a bilingual education or ESL program shall be determined by the language proficiency assessment committee in conjunction with the ARD committee in accordance with §89.1220(f) of this title (relating to Language Proficiency Assessment Committee).

(i) For exit from a bilingual education or ESL program, a student may be classified as English proficient only at the end of the school year in which a student would be able to participate equally in a general education, all-English instructional program. This determination shall be based upon all of the following:

(1) English proficiency on the state's approved test that measures the extent to which the student has developed oral and written language proficiency and specific language skills in English;

(2) passing standard met on the reading assessment instrument under the Texas Education Code (TEC), §39.023(a), or, for students at grade levels not assessed by the aforementioned reading assessment instrument, a score at or above the 40th percentile on both the English reading and the English language arts sections of the state's approved norm-referenced standardized achievement instrument; and

(3) English proficiency on a TEA-approved criterion-referenced written test and the results of a subjective teacher evaluation using the state's standardized rubric.

(j) A student may not be exited from the bilingual education or ESL program in prekindergarten or kindergarten. A school district must ensure that English learners are prepared to meet academic standards required by the TEC, §28.0211.

(k) A student may not be exited from the bilingual education or ESL program if the language proficiency assessment committee has recommended designated supports or accommodations on the state reading or writing assessment instrument.

(l) For English learners who are also eligible for special education services, the standardized process for English learner program exit is followed in accordance with applicable provisions of subsection (i) of this section. However, annual meetings to review student progress and make recommendations for program exit must be made in all instances by the language proficiency assessment committee in conjunction with the ARD committee in accordance with §89.1230(b) of this title (relating to Eligible

Students with Disabilities). Additionally, the language proficiency committee in conjunction with the ARD committee shall implement assessment procedures that differentiate between language proficiency and disabling conditions in accordance with §89.1230(a) of this title.

(m) For an English learner with significant cognitive disabilities, the language proficiency assessment committee in conjunction with the ARD committee may determine that the state's English language proficiency assessment for exit is not appropriate because of the nature of the student's disabling condition. In these cases, the language proficiency assessment committee in conjunction with the ARD committee may recommend that the student take the state's alternate English language proficiency assessment and shall determine an appropriate performance standard requirement for exit by language domain under subsection (i)(1) of this section;

(n) Notwithstanding §101.101 of this title (relating to Group-Administered Tests), all tests used for the purpose of identification, exit, and placement of students and approved by the TEA must be re-normed at least every eight years.

(o) The grade levels and the scores on each test that shall identify a student as an English learner or exit a student from a bilingual or ESL program shall be established by the TEA. The commissioner of education may review the approved list of tests, grade levels, and scores annually and update the list.

Statutory Authority: The provisions of this §89.1225 issued under the Texas Education Code, §§29.051, 29.053, 29.054, 29.055, 29.056, 29.0561, 29.057, 29.058, 29.059, 29.060, 29.061, 29.062, 29.063, 29.064, and 29.066.

Source: The provisions of this §89.1225 adopted to be effective September 1, 1996, 21 TexReg 5700; amended to be effective April 18, 2002, 27 TexReg 3107; amended to be effective September 17, 2007, 32 TexReg 6311; amended to be effective May 28, 2012, 37 TexReg 3822; amended to be effective July 15, 2018, 43 TexReg 4731.

§89.1226. Testing and Classification of Students, Beginning with School Year 2019-2020.

(a) Beginning with school year 2019-2020, the provisions of this subsection supersede the provisions in §89.1225 of this title (relating to Testing and Classification of Students).

(b) Within four weeks of initial enrollment in a Texas school, a student with a language other than English indicated on the home language survey shall be administered the state-approved English language proficiency test for identification as described in subsection (c) of this section and shall be identified as English learners and placed into the required bilingual education or ESL program in accordance with the criteria listed in subsection (f) of this section.

(c) For identifying English learners, school districts shall administer to each student who has a language other than English as identified on the home language survey:

(1) in prekindergarten through Grade 1, the listening and speaking components of the state-approved English language proficiency test for identification; and

(2) in Grades 2-12, the listening, speaking, reading, and writing components of the state-approved English language proficiency test for identification.

(d) School districts that provide a bilingual education program at the elementary grades shall administer a language proficiency test in the primary language of the student who is eligible to be served in the bilingual education program. If the primary language of the student is Spanish, the school district shall administer the Spanish version of the state-approved language proficiency test for identification. If a state-approved language proficiency test for identification is not available in the primary language of the student, the school district shall determine the student's level of proficiency using informal oral language assessment measures.

(e) All of the language proficiency testing shall be administered by professionals or paraprofessionals who are proficient in the language of the test and trained in the language proficiency testing requirements of the test publisher.

(f) For entry into a bilingual education or ESL program, a student shall be identified as an English learner using the following criteria.

(1) In prekindergarten through Grade 1, the student's score from the listening and speaking components on the state-approved English language proficiency test for identification is below the level designated for indicating English proficiency.

(2) In Grades 2-12, the student's score from the listening, speaking, reading, and writing components on the state-approved English language proficiency test for identification is below the level designated for indicating English proficiency.

(g) A student shall be identified as an English learner if the student's ability in English is so limited that the English language proficiency assessment described in subsection (c) of this section cannot be administered.

(h) The language proficiency assessment committee in conjunction with the admission, review, and dismissal (ARD) committee shall identify a student as an English learner if the student's ability in English is so limited or the student's disabilities are so severe that the English language proficiency assessment described in subsection (c) of this section cannot be administered. The decision for entry into a bilingual education or ESL program shall be determined by the language proficiency assessment committee in conjunction with the ARD committee in accordance with §89.1220(f) of this title (relating to Language Proficiency Assessment Committee).

(i) For exit from a bilingual education or ESL program, a student may be classified as English proficient only at the end of the school year in which a student would be able to participate equally in a general education, all-English instructional program. This determination shall be based upon all of the following:

(1) a proficiency rating on the state-approved English language proficiency test for exit that is designated for indicating English proficiency in each the four language domains (listening, speaking, reading, and writing);

(2) passing standard met on the reading assessment instrument under the Texas Education Code (TEC), §39.023(a), or, for students at grade levels not assessed by the aforementioned reading assessment instrument, a score at or above the 40th percentile on both the English reading and the English language arts sections of the state-approved norm-referenced standardized achievement instrument; and

(3) the results of a subjective teacher evaluation using the state's standardized rubric.

(j) A student may not be exited from the bilingual education or ESL program in prekindergarten or kindergarten. A school district must ensure that English learners are prepared to meet academic standards required by the TEC, §28.0211.

(k) A student may not be exited from the bilingual education or ESL program if the language proficiency assessment committee has recommended designated supports or accommodations on the state reading assessment instrument.

(l) For English learners who are also eligible for special education services, the standardized process for English learner program exit is followed in accordance with applicable provisions of subsection (i) of this section. However, annual meetings to review student progress and make recommendations for program exit must be made in all instances by the language proficiency assessment committee in conjunction with the ARD committee in accordance with §89.1230(b) of this title (relating to Eligible Students with Disabilities). Additionally, the language proficiency committee in conjunction with the ARD committee shall implement assessment procedures that differentiate between language proficiency and disabling conditions in accordance with §89.1230(a) of this title.

(m) For an English learner with significant cognitive disabilities, the language proficiency assessment committee in conjunction with the ARD committee may determine that the state's English language proficiency assessment for exit is not appropriate because of the nature of the student's disabling condition. In these cases, the language proficiency assessment committee in conjunction with the ARD committee may recommend that the student take the state's alternate English language proficiency assessment and shall determine an appropriate performance standard requirement for exit by language domain under subsection (i)(1) of this section;

(n) Notwithstanding §101.101 of this title (relating to Group-Administered Tests), all tests used for the purpose of identification, exit, and placement of students and approved by the TEA must be re-normed at least every eight years.

Statutory Authority: The provisions of this §89.1226 issued under the Texas Education Code, §§29.051, 29.053, 29.054, 29.055, 29.056, 29.0561, 29.057, 29.058, 29.059, 29.060, 29.061, 29.062, 29.063, 29.064, and 29.066.

Source: The provisions of this §89.1226 adopted to be effective September 1, 1996, 21 TexReg 5700; amended to be effective April 18, 2002, 27 TexReg 3107; amended to be effective September 17, 2007, 32 TexReg 6311; amended to be effective May 28, 2012, 37 TexReg 3822; amended to be effective July 1, 2019, 43 TexReg 4731.

§89.1227. Minimum Requirements for Dual Language Immersion Program Model.

(a) A dual language immersion program model shall address all curriculum requirements specified in Chapter 74, Subchapter A, of this title (relating to Required Curriculum) to include foundation and enrichment areas, English language proficiency standards, and college and career readiness standards.

(b) A dual language immersion program model shall be a full-time program of academic instruction in English and another language.

(c) A dual language immersion program model shall provide equitable resources in English and the additional program language whenever possible.

(d) A minimum of 50% of instructional time shall be provided in the language other than English for the duration of the program.

(e) Implementation shall:

(1) begin at prekindergarten or kindergarten, as applicable;

(2) continue without interruption incrementally through the elementary grades; and

(3) consider expansion to middle school and high school whenever possible.

(f) A dual language immersion program model shall be developmentally appropriate and based on current best practices identified in research.

Statutory Authority: The provisions of this §89.1227 issued under the Texas Education Code, §§29.051, 29.053, 29.054, 29.055, 29.056, 29.0561, 29.057, 29.058, 29.059, 29.060, 29.061, 29.062, 29.063, 29.064, and 29.066.

Source: The provisions of this §89.1227 adopted to be effective May 28, 2012, 37 TexReg 3822; amended to be effective July 15, 2018, 43 TexReg 4731.

§89.1228. Two-Way Dual Language Immersion Program Model Implementation.

(a) Student enrollment in a two-way dual language immersion program model is optional for English proficient students in accordance with §89.1233(a) of this title (relating to Participation of English Proficient Students).

(b) A two-way dual language immersion program model shall fully disclose candidate selection criteria and ensure that access to the program is not based on race, creed, color, religious affiliation, age, or disability.

(c) A school district implementing a two-way dual language immersion program model shall develop a policy on enrollment and continuation for students in this program model. The policy shall address:

  (1) eligibility criteria;

  (2) program purpose;

  (3) the district's commitment to providing equitable access to services for English learners;

  (4) grade levels in which the program will be implemented;

  (5) support of program goals as stated in §89.1210 of this title (relating to Program Content and Design); and

  (6) expectations for students and parents.

(d) A school district implementing a two-way program model shall obtain written parental approval as follows.

  (1) For English learners, written parental approval is obtained in accordance with §89.1240 of this title (relating to Parental Authority and Responsibility).

  (2) For English proficient students, written parental approval is obtained through a school district-developed process.

Statutory Authority: The provisions of this §89.1228 issued under the Texas Education Code, §§29.051, 29.053, 29.054, 29.055, 29.056, 29.0561, 29.057, 29.058, 29.059, 29.060, 29.061, 29.062, 29.063, 29.064, and 29.066.

Source: The provisions of this §89.1228 adopted to be effective May 28, 2012, 37 TexReg 3822; amended to be effective July 15, 2018, 43 TexReg 4731.

89.1229. General Standards for Recognition of Dual Language Immersion Program Models.

(a) School recognition. A school district may recognize one or more of its schools that implement an exceptional dual language immersion program model if the school meets all of the following criteria.

  (1) The school must meet the minimum requirements stated in §89.1227 of this title (relating to Minimum Requirements for Dual Language Immersion Program Model).

  (2) The school must receive an acceptable performance rating in the state accountability system.

  (3) The school must not be identified for any stage of intervention for the district's bilingual and/or English as a second language program under the performance-based monitoring system.

(b) Student recognition. A student participating in a dual language immersion program model or any other state-approved bilingual or ESL program model may be recognized by the program and its local school district board of trustees by earning a performance acknowledgement in accordance with §74.14 of this title (relating to Performance Acknowledgments).

Statutory Authority: The provisions of this §89.1229 issued under the Texas Education Code, §§29.051, 29.053, 29.054, 29.055, 29.056, 29.0561, 29.057, 29.058, 29.059, 29.060, 29.061, 29.062, 29.063, 29.064, and 29.066.

Source: The provisions of this §89.1229 adopted to be effective July 15, 2018, 43 TexReg 4731.

§89.1230. Eligible Students with Disabilities.

(a) School districts shall implement assessment procedures that differentiate between language proficiency and disabling conditions in accordance with Subchapter AA of this chapter (relating to Commissioner's Rules Concerning Special Education Services) and shall establish placement procedures that ensure that placement in a bilingual education or English as a second language program is not refused solely because the student has a disability.

(b) Language proficiency assessment committee members shall meet in conjunction with admission, review, and dismissal committee members to review and provide recommendations with regard to the educational needs of each English learner who qualifies for services in the special education program.

Statutory Authority: The provisions of this §89.1230 issued under the Texas Education Code, §§29.051, 29.053, 29.054, 29.055, 29.056, 29.0561, 29.057, 29.058, 29.059, 29.060, 29.061, 29.062, 29.063, 29.064, and 29.066.

Source: The provisions of this §89.1230 adopted to be effective September 1, 1996, 21 TexReg 5700; amended to be effective March 5, 1999, 24 TexReg 1383; amended to be effective May 28, 2012, 37 TexReg 3822; amended to be effective July 15, 2018, 43 TexReg 4731.

§89.1233. Participation of English Proficient Students.

(a) School districts shall fulfill their obligation to provide required bilingual program services to English learners in accordance with Texas Education Code (TEC), §29.053.

(b) School districts may enroll students who are not English learners in the bilingual education program or the English as a second language program in ac-cordance with TEC, §29.058.

(c) The number of participating students who are not English learners shall not exceed 40% of the number of students enrolled in the program district-wide in accordance with TEC, §29.058.

Statutory Authority: The provisions of this §89.1233 issued under the Texas Education Code, §§29.051, 29.053, 29.054, 29.055, 29.056, 29.0561, 29.057, 29.058, 29.059, 29.060, 29.061, 29.062, 29.063, 29.064, and 29.066.

Source: The provisions of this §89.1233 adopted to be effective March 5, 1999, 24 TexReg 1383 amended to be effective May 28, 2012, 37 TexReg 3822; amended to be effective July 15, 2018, 43 TexReg 4731.

§89.1235. Facilities.

Bilingual education and English as a second language (ESL) programs shall be located in the public schools of the school district with equitable access to all educational resources rather than in separate facilities. In order to provide the required bilingual education or ESL programs, school districts may concentrate the programs at a limited number of facilities within the school district. Recent immigrant English learners shall not remain enrolled in newcomer centers for longer than two years.

Statutory Authority: The provisions of this §89.1235 issued under the Texas Education Code, §§29.051, 29.053, 29.054, 29.055, 29.056, 29.0561, 29.057, 29.058, 29.059, 29.060, 29.061, 29.062, 29.063, 29.064, and 29.066.

Source: The provisions of this §89.1235 adopted to be effective September 1, 1996, 21 TexReg 5700; amended to be effective May 28, 2012, 37 TexReg 3822; amended to be effective July 15, 2018, 43 TexReg 4731.

§89.1240. Parental Authority and Responsibility.

(a) The parent or legal guardian shall be notified in English and the parent or legal guardian's primary language that their child has been classified as an English learner and recommended for placement in the required bilingual education or English as a second language (ESL) program. They shall be provided information describing the bilingual education or ESL program recommended, its benefits to the student, and its being an integral part of the school program to ensure that the parent or legal guardian understands the purposes and content of the program. The entry or placement of a student in the bilingual education or ESL program must be approved in writing by the student's parent or legal guardian in order to have the student included in the bilingual education allotment. The parent's or legal guardian's approval shall be considered valid for the student's continued participation in the required bilingual education or ESL program until the student meets the reclassification criteria described in §89.1225(i) of this title (relating to Testing and Classification of Students) or §89.1226(i) of this title (relating to Testing and Classification of Students, Beginning with School Year 2019-2020), the student graduates from high school, or a change occurs in program placement.

(b) The school district shall give written notification to the student's parent or legal guardian of the student's reclassification as English proficient and his or her exit from the bilingual education or ESL program and acquire written approval as required under the Texas Education Code, §29.056(a). Students meeting exit requirements may continue in the bilingual education or ESL program with parental approval but are not eligible for inclusion in the bilingual education allotment.

(c) The parent or legal guardian of a student enrolled in a school district that is required to offer bilingual education or ESL programs may appeal to the commissioner of education if the school district fails to comply with the law or the rules. Appeals shall be filed in accordance with Chapter 157 of this title (relating to Hearings and Appeals).

Statutory Authority: The provisions of this §89.1240 issued under the Texas Education Code, §§29.051, 29.053, 29.054, 29.055, 29.056, 29.0561, 29.057, 29.058, 29.059, 29.060, 29.061, 29.062, 29.063, 29.064, and 29.066.

Source: The provisions of this §89.1240 adopted to be effective September 1, 1996, 21 TexReg 5700; amended to be effective April 18, 2002, 27 TexReg 3107; amended to be effective May 28, 2012, 37 TexReg 3822; amended to be effective July 15, 2018, 43 TexReg 4731.

§89.1245. Staffing and Staff Development.

(a) School districts shall take all reasonable affirmative steps to assign appropriately certified teachers to the required bilingual education and English as a second language (ESL) programs in accordance with the Texas Education Code (TEC), §29.061, concerning bilingual education and special language program teachers. School districts that are unable to secure a sufficient number of appropriately certified bilingual education and/or ESL teachers to provide the required programs shall request activation of the appropriate permits in accordance with Chapter 230 of this title (relating to Professional Educator Preparation and Certification).

(b) School districts that are unable to employ a sufficient number of teachers, including part-time teachers, who meet the requirements of subsection (a) of this section for the bilingual education and ESL programs shall apply on or before November 1 for an exception to the bilingual education program as provided in §89.1207(a) of this title (relating to Bilingual Education Exceptions and English as a Second Language Waivers) or a waiver of the certification requirements in the ESL program as provided in §89.1207(b) of this title as needed.

(c) Teachers assigned to the bilingual education program and/or ESL program may receive salary supplements as authorized by the TEC, §42.153.

(d) School districts may compensate teachers and aides assigned to bilingual education and ESL programs for participation in professional development designed to increase their skills or lead to bilingual education or ESL certification.

(e) The commissioner of education shall encourage school districts to cooperate with colleges and universities to provide training for teachers assigned to the bilingual education and/or ESL programs.

(f) The Texas Education Agency shall develop, in collaboration with education service centers, resources for implementing bilingual education and ESL training programs. The materials shall provide a framework for:

(1) developmentally appropriate bilingual education programs for early childhood through the elementary grades;

(2) affectively, linguistically, and cognitively appropriate instruction in bilingual education and ESL programs in accordance with §89.1210(b)(1)-(3) of this title (relating to Program Content and Design); and

(3) developmentally appropriate programs for English learners identified as gifted and talented and English learners with disabilities.

Statutory Authority: The provisions of this §89.1245 issued under the Texas Education Code, §§29.051, 29.053, 29.054, 29.055, 29.056, 29.0561, 29.057, 29.058, 29.059, 29.060, 29.061, 29.062, 29.063, 29.064, and 29.066.

Source: The provisions of this §89.1245 adopted to be effective September 1, 1996, 21 TexReg 5700; amended to be effective March 5, 1999, 24 TexReg 1383; amended to be effective April 18, 2002, 27 TexReg 3107; amended to be effective May 28, 2012, 37 TexReg 3822; amended to be effective July 15, 2018, 43 TexReg 4731.

§89.1250. Required Summer School Programs.

Summer school programs that are provided under the Texas Education Code (TEC), §29.060, for English learners who will be eligible for admission to kindergarten or Grade 1 at the beginning of the next school year shall be implemented in accordance with this section.

(1) Purpose of summer school programs.

(A) English learners shall have an opportunity to receive special instruction designed to prepare them to be successful in kindergarten and Grade 1.

(B) Instruction shall focus on language development and essential knowledge and skills appropriate to the level of the student.

(C) The program shall address the affective, linguistic, and cognitive needs of the English learners in accordance with §89.1210(b) of this title (relating to Program Content and Design).

(2) Establishment of, and eligibility for, the program.

(A) Each school district required to offer a bilingual or English as a second language (ESL) program in accordance with the TEC, §29.053, shall offer the summer program.

(B) To be eligible for enrollment:

(i) a student must be eligible for admission to kindergarten or to Grade 1 at the beginning of the next school year and must be an English learner; and

(ii) a parent or guardian must have approved placement of the English learner in the required bilingual or ESL program following the procedures described in §89.1220(g) of this title (relating to Language Proficiency Assessment Committee) and §89.1225(b)-(f) of this title (relating to Testing and Classification of Students) or §89.1226(b)-(f) of this title (relating to Testing and Classification of Students, Beginning with School Year 2019-2020).

(3) Operation of the program.

(A) Enrollment is optional.

(B) The program shall be operated on a one-half day basis, a minimum of three hours each day, for eight weeks or the equivalent of 120 hours of instruction.

(C) The student/teacher ratio for the program district-wide shall not exceed 18 to one.

(D) A school district is not required to provide transportation for the summer program.

(E) Teachers shall possess certification as required in the TEC, §29.061, and §89.1245 of this title (relating to Staffing and Staff Development).

(F) Reporting of student progress shall be determined by the board of trustees. A summary of student progress shall be provided to parents at the conclusion of the program. This summary shall be provided to the student's teacher at the beginning of the next regular school term.

(G) A school district may join with other school districts in cooperative efforts to plan and implement programs.

(H) The summer school program shall not substitute for any other program required to be provided during the regular school term, including those required in the TEC, §29.153.

(4) Funding and records for programs.

(A) A school district shall use state and local funds for program purposes.

(i) Available funds appropriated by the legislature for the support of summer school programs provided under the TEC, §29.060, shall be allocated to school districts in accordance with this subsection.

(ii) Funding for the summer school program shall be on a unit basis in such an allocation system to ensure a pupil/teacher ratio of not more than 18 to one. The numbers of students required to earn units shall be established by the commissioner. The allotment per unit shall be determined by the commissioner based on funds available.

(iii) Any school district required to offer the program under paragraph (2)(A) of this subsection that has fewer than 10 students district-wide desiring to participate is not required to operate the program. However, those school districts must document that they have encouraged students' participation in multiple ways.

(iv) Payment to school districts for summer school programs shall be based on units employed. This information must be submitted in a manner and according to a schedule established by the commissioner in order for a school district to be eligible for funding.

(B) A school district shall maintain records of eligibility, attendance, and progress of students.

Statutory Authority: The provisions of this §89.1250 issued under the Texas Education Code, §§29.051, 29.053, 29.054, 29.055, 29.056, 29.0561, 29.057, 29.058, 29.059, 29.060, 29.061, 29.062, 29.063, 29.064, and 29.066.

Source: The provisions of this §89.1250 adopted to be effective September 1, 1996, 21 TexReg 5700; amended to be effective April 18, 2002, 27 TexReg 3107; amended to be effective February 17, 2005, 30 TexReg 709; amended to be effective September 17, 2007, 32 TexReg 6311; amended to be effective May 28, 2012, 37 TexReg 3822; amended to be effective July 15, 2018, 43 TexReg 4731.

§89.1265. Evaluation.

(a) All school districts required to conduct a bilingual education or English as a second language (ESL) program shall conduct an annual evaluation in accordance with Texas Education Code (TEC), §29.053, collecting a full range of data to determine program effectiveness to ensure student academic success. The annual evaluation report shall be presented to the board of trustees before November 1 of each year and the report shall be retained at the school district level in accordance with TEC, §29.062.

(b) Annual school district reports of educational performance shall reflect:

(1) the academic progress in the language(s) of instruction for English learners;

(2) the extent to which English learners are becoming proficient in English;

(3) the number of students who have been exited from the bilingual education and ESL programs; and

(4) the number of teachers and aides trained and the frequency, scope, and results of the professional development in approaches and strategies that support second language acquisition.

(c) In addition, for those school districts that filed in the previous year and/or will be filing a bilingual education exception and/or ESL waiver in the current year, the annual district report of educational performance shall also reflect:

(1) the number of teachers for whom an exception or waiver was/is being filed;

(2) the number of teachers for whom an exception or waiver was filed in the previous year who successfully obtained certification; and

(3) the frequency and scope of a comprehensive professional development plan, implemented as required under §89.1207 of this title (relating to Bilingual Education Exceptions and English as a Second Language Waivers), and results of such plan if an exception and/or waiver was filed in the previous school year.

(d) School districts shall report to parents the progress of their child in acquiring English as a result of participation in the program offered to English learners.

(e) Each school year, the principal of each school campus, with the assistance of the campus level committee, shall develop, review, and revise the campus improvement plan described in the TEC, §11.253, for the purpose of improving student performance for English learners.

Statutory Authority: The provisions of this §89.1265 issued under the Texas Education Code, §§29.051, 29.053, 29.054, 29.055, 29.056, 29.0561, 29.057, 29.058, 29.059, 29.060, 29.061, 29.062, 29.063, 29.064, and 29.066.

Source: The provisions of this §89.1265 adopted to be effective September 1, 1996, 21 TexReg 5700; amended to be effective April 18, 2002, 27 TexReg 3107; amended to be effective May 28, 2012, 37 TexReg 3822; amended to be effective July 15, 2018, 43 TexReg 4731.

Bibliography

Asher, J. (1969). The total physical response approach to second language learning. *The Modern Language Journal, 53(1)*, 3-17.

Atwell, N. (2007). *The reading zone: How to help kids become skilled, passionate, habitual, critical readers*. New York, NY: Scholastic Teaching Resources.

August, D., & Shanahan, T. (2006). *Developing literacy in a second language: Report of the National Literacy Panel*. Mahwah, NJ: Lawrence Erlbaum.

August, D., & Shanahan, D. (2010). Effective English literacy instruction for English learners. In *Improving education for English learners: Research-based approaches* (pp. 209–249). Sacramento, CA: California Department of Education.

August, D., & Shanahan, T. (2010). Response to a review and update on developing literacy in second-language learners: Report of the National Literacy Panel on language minority children and youth. *Journal of Literacy Research, 42(3)*, 341-348.

Ausubel, D. P. (1960). The use of advance organizers in the learning and retention of meaningful verbal material. *Journal of Educational Psychology, 51*(5), 267.

Baker, L. (2004). Reading comprehension and science inquiry: Metacognitive connections. In W. Saul (Ed.). *Crossing borders in literacy and science instruction: Perspectives on theory and practice*. Arlington, VA: National Science Teachers Association.

Barth, R. S. (2002). *Learning by heart*. San Francisco, CA: Jossey-Bass.

Bauman, J. F., Jones, L. A., & Seifert-Kessell, N. (1993). *Monitoring reading comprehension by thinking aloud (Instructional Resource No. 1)*. Athens, GA: University of Georgia, National Reading Research Center.

Bear, D. R., Invernizzi, M., Templeton, S., & Johnston, F. (2000). *Words their way: Word study for phonics, vocabulary, and spelling instruction* (2nd ed.). Upper Saddle River, NJ: Prentice-Hall.

Beck, I. L., McKeown, M. G., Hamilton, R. L., & Kugan, L. (1997). *Questioning the author: An approach for enhancing student engagement with text*. Newark, DE: International Reading Association.

Berg, E. C. (1999). The effects of trained peer response on ESL students' revision types and writing quality. *Journal of Second Language Writing, 8(3)*, 215-241.

Boulware, B. J., & Crow, M. L. (2008). Using the concept attainment strategy to enhance reading comprehension. *The Reading Teacher, 61(6)*, 491-495.

Brown, A. L., Campione, J. C., & Day, J. D. (1981). Learning to learn: On training students to learn from texts. *Educational Researcher, 10(2)*, 14-21.

Bruner, J. S., Goodnow, J. J., & Austin, G. A. (1956). *A study of thinking*. New York, NY: Wiley.

Bruner, J. S., & Kalnins, I. V. (1973). The coordination of visual observation and instrumental behavior in early infancy. *Perception, 2,* 307-314.

Callow, J. (2008). Show me: Principles for assessing students' visual literacy. *The Reading Teacher, 61(8)*, 616-626.

Castillo, M. J. (2012). *Guiding educators to praxis: Moving teachers beyond theory to practice*. ProQuest LLC, Ed.D. Dissertation, Arizona State University.

Celce-Murcia, M., Brinton, D. M., & Goodwin, J. M. (2010). *Teaching pronunciation hardback with audio CDs (2): A course book and reference guide.* Cambridge: Cambridge University Press.

Chamot, A. U., & O'Malley, J. M. (1994). *The CALLA handbook: Implementing the cognitive academic language learning approach.* Boston, MA: Addison-Wesley.

Chamot, A. U. (2004). Issues in language learning strategy research and teaching. *Electronic Journal of Foreign Language Teaching, 1(1),* 14-26. Retrieved from: http://e-flt.nus.edu.sg/v1n12004/chamot.pdf

Csikszentmihalyi, M. (1990). *Flow: The psychology of optimal experience.* New York, NY: Harper & Row.

Daniels, H. (1994). *Literature circles: Voice and choice in the student-centered classroom.* York, ME: Stenhouse Publishers.

Davis, L. L., & O'Neill, R. E. (2004). Use of response cards with a group of students with learning disabilities including those for whom English is a second language. J*ournal of Applied Behavior Analysis, 37(2),* 219-222.

Dean, D. (1986). Questioning techniques for teachers: A closer look at the process. *Contemporary Education, 57(4),* 184-85.

Diamond, L., & Gutlohn, L. (2006). *Vocabulary handbook.* Baltimore, MD: Brookes.

Dole, J. A., Duffy, G. G., Roehler, L. R., & Pearson, P. D. (1991). Moving from the old to the new: Research on reading comprehension instruction. *Review of Educational Research, 61(2),* 239-264.

Duffy, G. G. (2002). The case for direct explanation of strategies. In C. C. Block & M. Pressley (Eds.), *Comprehension instruction* (pp. 28–41). New York, NY: Guilford.

Dutro, S. & Moran, C. (2003). Rethinking English language instruction: An architectural approach. In G. G. Garcia (Ed.), *English learners: Reaching the highest level of English literacy* (pp. 227-258). Newark, DE: International Reading Association.

Dutro, S. & Kinsella, K. (2010). English language development: issues and implementation in grades 6–12. In California Department of Education (Ed.), *Improving education for English learners: Research-based approaches* (pp. 151–207). Sacramento, CA: CDE Press.

Echevarria, J., & Graves, A. (2015). Sheltered content instruction: *Teaching English language learners with diverse abilities.* Boston, MA: Pearson.

Echevarria, J., Vogt, M., & Short, D. (2017). *Making content comprehensible for English learners: The SIOP Model, (5th ed.).* New York, NY: Pearson.

Elbow, P. (1998). *Writing with power: Techniques for mastering the writing process.* New York, NY: Oxford University Press.

Escamilla, K., Soltero-González, L., Butvilofsky, S., Hopewell, S., & Sparrow, W. (2010). *Transitions to biliteracy: Literacy squared.* Boulder, CO: University of Colorado.

Eyraud, K., Giles, G., Koenig, S., & Stoller, F. L. (2000). The word wall approach: Promoting L2 vocabulary learning. *English Teaching Forum Online 38(3),* 3.

Faltis, C. (1992). Programmatic and curricular options for secondary schools serving limited English proficient students. *The High School Journal, 76(2),* 171-181. Retrieved from http://www.jstor.org/stable/40364562

Fisher, D., & Frey, N. (2007). *Checking for understanding: Formative assessment techniques for your classroom.* Alexandria, VA: ASCD.

Florez, M. C. (1998). *Improving adult ESL learners' pronunciation skills.* ERIC, National Clearinghouse for ESL Literacy Education. Retrieved from: https://files.eric.ed.gov/fulltext/ED427553.pdf

Fountas, I. C., & Pinnell, G. S. (2001). *Guiding readers and writers, grades 3-6: Teaching comprehension, genre, and content literacy.* Portsmouth, NH: Heinemann.

Gall, M. (1984). Synthesis of research on teachers' questioning. *Educational Leadership, 42(3),* 40-47.

Gibbons, P. (2002). *Scaffolding language, scaffolding learning: Teaching second language learners in the mainstream classroom.* Portsmouth, NH: Heinemann.

Goldenberg, C. (1992). Instructional conversations: Promoting comprehension through discussion. *The Reading Teacher, 46(4),* 316-326.

Goldenberg, C., & Coleman, R. (2010). *Promoting academic achievement among English learners: A guide to the research.* Thousand Oaks, CA: Corwin Press.

Hakuta, K., Butler, Y. G., & Witt, D. (2000). How long does it take English learners to attain proficiency? *The University of California Linguistic Minority Research Institute Policy Report, 2001.* Retrieved December, 2017 from: http://repositories.cdlib.org/lmri/pr/hakuta/

Harrington, M. J. (1996). Basic instruction in word analysis skills to improve spelling competence. *Education, 117(1),* 22-31.

Hauser, J. A. (1990). *Classroom discourse: Questions, quarrels, and introspections.* Distributed by ERIC Clearinghouse. Retrieved from: https://www.researchgate.net/publication/234707421

Head, M. H., & Readence, J. E. (1986). Anticipation guides: Enhancing meaning through prediction. In E. K. Dishner, T. W. Bean, J. E. Readence, & D. W. Moore (Eds.), *Reading in the content areas: Improving classroom instruction (2nd ed.)* (pp. 229–234). Dubuque, IA: Kendall/Hunt.

High, J. (1993). *Second language learning through cooperative learning (Vol. 1).* San Clemente, CA: Kagan Publishing.

Hill, J., & Flynn, K. (2006). *Classroom instruction that works with English language learners.* Alexandria, VA: Association for Supervision and Curriculum Development.

Information on State Assessments for English Language Learners. (n.d.). Retrieved December 11, 2017, from https://tea.texas.gov/student.assessment/ell/

Izumi, S. (2002). Output, input enhancement, and the noticing hypothesis. *Studies in Second Language Acquisition, 24(4),* 541-577.

Johnson, D. W., & Johnson, R. T. (1995). *Creative controversy: Intellectual challenge in the classroom (3rd ed.).* Edina, MN: Interaction Book Company.

Kagan, S. (1990). Cooperative learning for students limited in language proficiency. In M. Brubacher, R. Payne, & K. Rickett (Eds.), *Perspectives on small group learning* (pp. 202-223). Oakville, Ontario, Canada: Rubicon Publishing, Inc.

Kagan, S. (1992). *Cooperative learning.* San Juan Capistrano, CA: Kagan Cooperative Learning.

Kirschner, P. A., Sweller, J., & Clark, R. E. (2006). Why minimal guidance during instruction does not work: An analysis of the failure of constructivist, discovery, problem-based, experiential, and inquiry-based teaching. *Educational Psychologist, 41(2)*, 75-86.

Knapp, F. A., & Desrochers, M. N. (2009). An experimental evaluation of the instructional effectiveness of a student response system: Comparison with constructed overt responding. *International Journal of Teaching and Learning in Higher Education, 21(1)*, 36-46.

Krashen, S. (1982). *Principles and practice in second language acquisition.* New York, NY: Pergamon.

Leeman, J. (2003). Recasts and second language development. *Studies in Second Language Acquisition, 25(1)*, 37-63.

Long, M. (1996). The role of the linguistic environment in second language acquisition. In W. Ritchie, & T. Bhatia (Eds.), *Handbook of second language acquisition: Vol 2.* (pp. 413-468). San Diego, CA: Academic Press.

Long, M. (2007). *Problems in SLA.* Mahwah, NJ: Lawrence Erlbaum Associates.

Lyman, F. (1981). The responsive classroom discussion: The inclusion of all students. *Mainstreaming Digest* (pp. 109-113). College Park, MD: University of Maryland.

Maccini, P., & Gagnon, J. C. (2000). Best practices for teaching mathematics to secondary students with special needs: Implications from teacher perceptions and a review of the literature. *Focus on Exceptional Children, 32(5)*, 1.

Macon, J., Bewell, D., & Vogt, M. (1991). *Responses to literature.* Newark. DE: International Reading Association.

Manzo, A. V. (1969). The request procedure. *Journal of Reading, 13(2)*, 123-126.

Marzano, R. (2004). *Building background knowledge for academic achievement: Research on what works in schools.* Alexandria, VA: ASCD.

Marzano, R. J., Pickering, D., & Pollock, J. E. (2001). *Classroom instruction that works: Research-based strategies for increasing student achievement.* Alexandria, VA: ASCD.

Maurice, K. (1983). The fluency workshop. *TESOL Newsletter, 17(4)*, 29.

Mayer, R. E. (2003). *Learning and instruction.* Upper Saddle River, NJ: Pearson Education, Inc.

Meiers, M. (Ed.). (2006). *Teachers' stories: Professional standards, professional learning: Using STELLA as a framework for professional learning.* South Australia: Australian Literacy Educators' Association (ALEA).

Meyen, E., Vergason, G., & Whelan, R. (1996). *Strategies for teaching exceptional children in inclusive settings.* Denver, CO: Love Publishing Company.

McLaughlin, M. (2003). *Guided comprehension in the primary grades.* Newark. DE: International Reading Association.

Morgenstern, L. (1992). Action and inaction: Student and teacher roles in classroom participation. Michigan Technological University. ERIC Document Reproduction Service No. ED 346 534.

Morse, O. (2011). SOAPSTone: A Strategy for Reading and Writing. New York, NY: College Board.

Motley, N. (2016) *Talk, read, talk, write (2nd ed.).* Irving, TX Seidlitz Education.

National Center for Science Education (NCSE). Polling American Scientific Literacy. Retrieved April 24, 2013, from http://ncse.com/news/2013/04/polling-american-scientificliteracy-0014818

National Council of Teachers of English (NCTE). (2008). Policy research brief: English language learners. The James R. Squire Office for Policy Research. Retrieved from http://www.ncte.org/library/NCTEFiles/Resources/PolicyResearch/ELLResearchBrief.pdf

Nell, V. (1988). *Lost in a book: The psychology of reading for pleasure.* New Haven, CT: Yale University Press.

Norris, J. M., & Ortega, L. (2000). Effectiveness of L2 instruction: A research synthesis and quantitative meta-analysis. *Language Learning, 50(3),* 417-528.

Novak, J. D. (1995). Concept mapping: A strategy for organizing knowledge. In S. M. Glynn, & R. Duit (Eds.). *Learning science in the schools: Research reforming practice* (pp. 229-245). Mahwah, NJ: Lawrence Erlbaum Associates, Inc.

Ogle, D. M. (1986). KWL: A teaching model that develops active reading of expository text. *The Reading Teacher, 39(6),* 564-570.

Oxford, R., & Nyikos, M. (1989). Variables affecting choice of language learning strategies by university students. *The Modern Language Journal, 73(3),* 291-300.

Palincsar, A. S., & Brown, A. L. (1985). Reciprocal teaching: Activities to promote read(ing) with your mind. In T. L. Harris, & E. J. Cooper (Eds.), *Reading, thinking and concept development: Strategies for the classroom.* New York, NY: College Board.

Pauk, W. (2013). *How to study in college.* Boston, MA: Wadsworth Cengage Learning.

Pilgreen, J. L. (2000). *The SSR handbook: How to organize and manage a sustained silent reading program.* Portsmouth, NH: Boynton/Cook Publishers.

Powell, M. (1996). *Presenting in English: How to give successful presentations.* Hove, UK: Language Teaching Publications.

Ruddell, M. R., & Shearer, B. A. (2002). "Extraordinary," "tremendous," "exhilarating," "magnificent": Middle school at-risk students become avid word learners with the vocabulary self-collection strategy (VSS). *Journal of Adolescent and Adult Literacy, 45(4),* 352-363.

Samway, K. D. (2006). *When English language learners write: Connecting research to practice, K-8.* Portsmouth, NH: Heinemann.

Saunders, W., Goldenberg, C., & Marcelletti, D. (2013). English language development: Guidelines for instruction. *American Educator, 37(2),* 13–25, 38–39.

Schmidt, R. W. (2001). Attention. In P. Robinson (Ed.), *Cognition and second language instruction (pp. 3-32).* New York, NY: Cambridge University Press.

Schmidt, R. (2010). Attention, awareness, and individual differences in language learning. In W. M. Chan, S. Chi, K. N. Cin, J. Istanto, M. Nagami, J. W. Sew, T. Suthiwan, & I. Walker, *Proceedings of CLaSIC 2010,* Singapore, December 2-4, 721-737. Singapore: National University of Singapore, Centre for Language Studies.

Schlick Noe, K., & Johnson, N. (1999). *Getting started with literature circles.* Norwood, MA: Christopher-Gordon Publishers, Inc.

Seidlitz, J., & Castillo, M. (2010). *Language & literacy for ELLs workbook.* Irving, TX: Seidlitz Education.

Seidlitz, J. (2011). *Sheltered instruction plus: A comprehensive plan for successfully teaching English language learners.* Irving, TX: Seidlitz Education.

Seidlitz, J., & Perryman, B. (2011). *7 steps to a language-rich, interactive classroom: Research-based strategies for engaging all students.* Irving, TX: Seidlitz Education.

Seidlitz, J., & Castillo, M. (2013). *Language and literacy for ELLs: Creating a systematic change for academic language.* Irving, TX: Seidlitz Education.

Seidlitz, J., Base, M., Lara, M., Rodríguez, M., & Hartill, M. (2015). *ELLs in Texas: What administrators need to know (2nd ed.).* Irving, TX: Seidlitz Education.

Seidlitz, J., Base, M., Lara, M., & Smith, H. (2016). *ELLs in Texas: What teachers need to know.* Irving, TX: Seidlitz Education.

Snow, C. E., Griffin, P., & Burns, M. S. (2005). *Knowledge to support the teaching of reading: Preparing teachers for a changing world.* San Francisco, CA: Jossey-Bass.

Swain, M. (1995). Three functions of output in second language learning. In G. Cook, & B. Seidlhofer (Eds.), Principle and practice in applied linguistics: *Studies in honour of H. G. Widdowson* (pp. 125-144). Oxford: Oxford University Press.

Taba, H. (1967). *Teachers' handbook for elementary social studies. Reading,* MA: Addison-Wesley.

Taylor, W. L. (1953). Cloze procedure: A new tool for measuring readability. *Journalism Bulletin, 30(4),* 415-433.

Thornbury, S. (2005). *How to teach speaking.* Harlow, England: Longman.

Vail, N. J., & Papenfuss, J. F. (1993). *Daily oral language plus: Level 3.* Boston, MA: McDougal, Littell & Company.

Watanabe, Y., & Swain, M. (2007). Effects of proficiency differences and patterns of pair interaction on second language learning: Collaborative dialogue between adult ESL learners. *Language Teaching Research, 11(2),* 121-142.

Weaver, C. (1996). *Teaching grammar in context.* Portsmouth, NH: Boynton/Cook Publishers.

Wennerstrom, A. (1993). Content vs. function. Content-based pronunciation. *TESOL Journal, 1(3),* 15-18.

White, T., Sowell, J., & Yanagihara, A. (1989). Teaching elementary students to use word-part clues. *The Reading Teacher, (42)4,* 302-308.

Wilhem, J. (2002). *Action strategies for deepening comprehension.* New York, NY: Scholastic Professional Books.

Wilkinson, A, (1970). The concept of oracy. *The English Journal, 59(1),* 71-77.

Zwiers, J. (2008). *Building academic language.* Newark, DE: Jossey-Bass/International Reading Association.

JOHN SEIDLITZ is an independent educational consultant and the author of *Sheltered Instruction in Texas: A Guide for Teachers of ELLs; Navigating the ELPS: Using the New Standards to Improve Instruction for English Learners;* and a contributing author for The SIOP® Model for Teaching History-Social Studies for English Learners.

He is the co-author of numerous publications including the *7 Steps to a Language-Rich, Interactive Classroom*® and *ELLs in Texas: What Administrators Need to Know.* Mr. Seidlitz has been a member of the SIOP® National faculty and guest lecturer for many regional and national language development conferences.

He taught social studies and ESL, served as a secondary ESL program coordinator, and held the position of education specialist at ESC Region 20 in San Antonio, Texas. In 2005, Mr. Seidlitz founded Seidlitz Education which is dedicated to the mission of Giving Kids the Gift of Academic Language™.

Three ways to order

- **FAX** completed order form with payment information to **(949) 200-4384**
- **PHONE** order information to **(210) 315-7119**
- **ORDER ONLINE** at **www.seidlitzeducation.com**

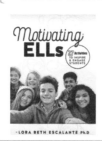
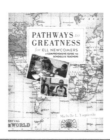

TITLE	PRICE	QTY	TOTAL$	TITLE	PRICE	QTY	TOTAL$
NEW! 7 Steps To a Language-Rich, Interactive **Foreign Language** Classroom	$32.95			7 Pasos para crear un aula interactiva y rica en lenguaje SPANISH	$29.95		
NEW! Boosting Achievement: Reaching Students with Interrupted or Minimal Education	$26.95			38 Great Academic Language Builders	$24.95		
NEW! Motivating ELLs: 27 Activities to Inspire & Engage Students	$26.95			Diverse Learner Flip Book	$26.95		
NEW! Pathways to Greatness for ELL Newcomers: A Comprehensive Guide for Schools & Teachers	$32.95			ELLs in Texas: What Teachers Need to Know 2ND EDITION	$34.95		
NEW! Sheltered Instruction in Texas: Second Language Acquisition Methods for Teachers of ELs	$29.95			ELLs in Texas: What Administrators Need to Know 2ND EDITION	$29.95		
NEW! Talk Read Talk Write: A Practical Routine for Learning in All Content Areas K-12 2ND EDITION	$32.95			ELPS Flip Book	$19.95		
NEW! Teaching Social Studies to ELLs	$24.95			Navigating the ELPS: Using the Standards to Improve Instruction for English Learners	$24.95		
NEW! Teaching Science to English Learners	$24.95			Navigating the ELPS: Math (2nd Edition)	$29.95		
NEW! ¡Toma la Palabra! SPANISH	$32.95			Navigating the ELPS: Science	$29.95		
NEW! Mi Cuaderno de Dictado SPANISH	$7.95			Navigating the ELPS: Social Studies	$29.95		
7 Steps to a Language-Rich Interactive Classroom	$29.95			Navigating the ELPS: Language Arts and Reading	$34.95		
				RTI for ELLs Fold-Out	$16.95		
				Vocabulary Now! 44 Strategies All Teachers Can Use	$29.95		
COLUMN 1 TOTAL $				COLUMN 2 TOTAL $			

COLUMN 1+2	$
DISCOUNT	$
SHIPPING	$
TAX	$
TOTAL	$

Pricing, specifications, and availability subject to change without notice.

SHIPPING 9% of order total, minimum $14.95
5-7 business days to ship. If needed sooner please call for rates.
TAX EXEMPT? please fax a copy of your certificate along with order.

NAME

SHIPPING ADDRESS   CITY   STATE, ZIP

PHONE NUMBER   EMAIL ADDRESS

TO ORDER BY FAX
to **(949) 200-4384**
please complete
credit card info *or*
attach purchase order

☐ Visa   ☐ MasterCard   ☐ Discover   ☐ AMEX

CARD #   EXPIRES
          mm/yyyy
SIGNATURE   CVV
          3- or 4- digit code

☐ **Purchase Order attached**
please make P.O. out to **Seidlitz Education**

For information about Seidlitz Education products and professional development, please contact us at

(210) 315-7119 | kathy@johnseidlitz.com
56 Via Regalo, San Clemente, CA 92673
www.seidlitzeducation.com

Giving kids the gift of **academic language.**™

REV061419

SEIDLITZ PRODUCT ORDER FORM

Three ways to order

- **FAX** completed order form with payment information to **(949) 200-4384**
- **PHONE** order information to **(210) 315-7119**
- **ORDER ONLINE** at **www.seidlitzeducation.com**

Pricing, specifications, and availability subject to change without notice.

TITLE	Price	QTY	TOTAL $
NEW! *Instead Of I Don't Know* Poster For the LOTE Classroom 24" x 36"			
☐ LOTE FRENCH	$9.95		
☐ LOTE SPANISH	$9.95		
☐ LOTE GERMAN	$9.95		
TOTAL $			

TITLE	Price	QTY	TOTAL $
Academic Language Cards and Activity Booklet, ENGLISH	$19.95		
Academic Language Cards, SPANISH	$9.95		
TOTAL $			

TITLE	Price	QTY	TOTAL $
Instead Of I Don't Know Poster, 24" x 36"			
☐ Elementary ENGLISH	$9.95		
☐ Secondary ENGLISH	$9.95		
20 pack *Instead Of I Don't Know* Posters, 11" x 17"			
☐ Elementary ENGLISH	$40.00		
☐ Secondary ENGLISH	$40.00		
Instead Of I Don't Know Poster, 24" x 36" Elementary SPANISH	$9.95		
20 pack *Instead Of I Don't Know* Posters, 11" x 17" Elementary SPANISH	$40.00		
TOTAL $			

	TITLE	Price	QTY	TOTAL $
Please speak in complete sentences.	*Please Speak In Complete Sentences* Poster 24" x 36" ☐ ENGLISH ☐ SPANISH	$9.95		
	20 pack *Please Speak In Complete Sentences* Posters, 11" x 17" ☐ ENGLISH ☐ SPANISH	$40.00		
	TOTAL $			

SHIPPING 9% of order total, minimum $14.95
5-7 business days to ship.
If needed sooner please call for rates.

TAX EXEMPT? please fax a copy of your certificate along with order.

GRAND TOTAL	$
DISCOUNT	$
SHIPPING	$
TAX	$
FINAL TOTAL	$

NAME

SHIPPING ADDRESS   CITY   STATE, ZIP

PHONE NUMBER   EMAIL ADDRESS

TO ORDER BY FAX
to **(949) 200-4384**
please complete
credit card info **or**
attach purchase order

☐ Visa ☐ MasterCard ☐ Discover ☐ AMEX

CARD #   EXPIRES   mm/yyyy

SIGNATURE   CVV

☐ **Purchase Order attached**
please make
P.O. out to
Seidlitz Education